Allerd Stikker (1928) obtained an MSc degree in Chemical Engineering from Delft University of Technology (1953) and then held various positions in the international corporate sector, including executive member of the boards of AKZO and RSV. In 1986, he obtained an MA degree in Theology and Religious Studies from Leeds University. From 1990 to 2010, he ran the Ecological Management Foundation (EMF), where he focused on putting into practice a closer coherence between ecology and economy. Since the beginning of the 21st century, EMF has been involved in the large-scale application of sustainable, small-scale solutions to clean water scarcity in developing countries. Having passed the management of EMF to a new, younger generation, he set up the Valley Foundation in 2010 with the aim of enhancing social and technological innovation in the water sphere. At present, he still serves on the boards of the Alliance of Religions and Conservation (ARC) and Voltea Ltd., a water technology company in the Unilever Ventures portfolio. In previous periods, he published a number of books, including *The Transformation Factor: Towards Ecological Consciousness* (1992), *Closing the Gap: Exploring the History of Gender Relations* (2002) and *Water: The Blood of the Earth* (2007).

Allerd Stikker

Three Windows on Eternity

Exploring Evolution and Human Destiny

Illustrated by Rosa Vitalie

WATKINS PUBLISHING
LONDON

This edition first published in the UK and USA 2013 by
Watkins Publishing Limited, Sixth Floor,
75 Wells Street, London W1T 3QH

A member of Osprey Group

Originally published by Wereldbibliotheek (Amsterdam) in 2012 as En de mens speelt met de tijd.

10 9 8 7 6 5 4 3 2 1

Typeset by Bookcraft, Stroud, Gloucestershire

Printed and bound in Italy by L.E.G.O. S.p.A.

A CIP record for this book is available from the British Library

ISBN: 978-1-78028-596-2

www.watkinspublishing.co.uk

Distributed in the USA and Canada by Sterling Publishing Co., Inc.
387 Park Avenue South, New York, NY 10016-8810

For information about custom editions, special sales, premium and
corporate purchases, please contact Sterling Special Sales Department at 800-805 5489 or
specialsales@sterlingpub.com

Contents

1
Background

What is the essence of life and of the world around us? What is our role as human beings and how did we get here? Anyone who ever wonders at the magic, the variety as well as the harshness and complexity of life will encounter these questions from time to time. Some people find the answers in religion or spirituality while others find them in philosophy or science. And still others feel their heads spinning and prefer to go back to their daily rituals.

During my many travels through life, I kept running into a riddle that has occupied so many people in the history of our existence: the riddle of creation. Ever since my days as a student at Delft University of Technology, which began in 1946, I have been utterly amazed by the wonders of creation, by its forms, its colours, its sounds and its moods. The chemical engineering programme at Delft did not pay any attention to such things.

An incident
A seemingly trivial event made me realise the difference between what I was learning in Delft and what happens in creation. It was during a project lasting many weeks in the organic chemistry laboratory, where I had to make a complex organic dye from a number of chemical ingredients. This was achieved through chemical reactions, often under high temperature and pressure, using various separation techniques. It was all done on the basis of carefully derived chemical formulae and equations.

As I was plodding my way through this task, I arrived home one evening and noticed that a beautifully coloured flower had started growing that day in a flowerpot in my room. It had appeared just like that – from earth and water, air and light, at room temperature and atmospheric pressure, without a manual and without any equipment – as a pure, complex, organic dye. It then became clear to me that the technological world and the natural world are not one and the same. I became aware of an invisible coherence in creation.

In search of that coherence while still in my early twenties, I did not get much further than the discovery that there were contradictions between the measurability, computability, predictability and controllability of the material world revolving around technology and science, on the one hand, and the mysteries and wonders of nature, on the other. I discovered that the concept of natural science is actually a contradiction in terms.

Later, in my thirties – with a profession, a career, a family and social involvement – the same dualistic experience resurfaced when, in 1963, I read Le Phénomène Humain (The Phenomenon of Man) by Pierre Teilhard de Chardin. The book addresses the relationship between material and non-material phenomena in the evolution of the cosmos.

I was surprised and dazzled by the magnificent cosmological process of evolution described in detail by Teilhard de Chardin, which is still going on today. He dubbed it cosmogenesis, a demonstrable process by which matter evolves to ever more complex forms and ever higher degrees of consciousness. I became curious about the nature and progress of this evolutionary process and the relationship between the rational and non-rational aspects of my environment.

Journey of discovery

I then started looking for a fulfilling view of the world and a better understanding of my role and the role of human society in the evolution in creation. By creation I mean everything within me, around me, before me, after me, without me – the whole universe and beyond. And by evolution I mean the whole process, starting with the emergence of the universe 13.5 billion years ago all the way up to the present day.

The majestic story of creation and of evolution is not always a happy tale. It is not only about creativity and continuity but also about decline and discontinuity, with the ups and downs familiar in our own lives.

Based on what we now know about the 13.5-billion-year history of evolution in creation, I have become aware of the magnificent edifice which in the course of time has grown from a mix of emergence and development, chance and choice, as well as mystery and mutation.

To individual human beings, the evolution in creation manifests itself through four worlds they experience.

I have also come to realise that the evolution in creation is filled with mysteries which are invariably accompanied by radical discontinuities. Science is unable to explain these mysteries. The discontinuities in the evolutionary process can apparently not be predicted nor explained. At best, they can be demonstrated but not until after the event. Here, science has arrived at the boundary of what is measurable.

The three major mysteries in the evolution within creation – the emergence of the universe, the emergence of life and the emergence of self-reflective consciousness – confront us with wonder, surprise, consistent patterns and unexpected innovations. Studying the course of these three mysteries has made me see that creation is linked to eternity and evolution is linked to time. My awareness of a link between creation and evolution – between eternity and time – gives me peace in creation and inspiration in evolution.

To individual human beings, the evolution in creation manifests itself through four worlds they experience. These are the worlds in and through which we live and exist, but which are not generally experienced as a single interconnected whole. They are the macro world of the stars and planets from which we originate, the micro world of the molecules from which we are made, the meso world of our busy daily lives, and the meta world of reflection and spirituality. A coherent world view requires that we experience these worlds as an integral whole. If we exclude or ignore one of these worlds, that world view will be distorted.

An integral experience of the four worlds was originally the role of religion, and this role is still very important. But the world today – where new generations think differently and ancient texts are far removed from their present environment – also requires a new and coherent story. This story should be in harmony with new lifestyles and current scientific knowledge. It should provide inspiration for a meaningful and practical outlook on life both today and tomorrow.

> I believe in creation in eternity rather than in a Creator in time.

In my own case, the new tale should include the notion that everything in the evolution in creation originated from within and not from without. I believe in creation in eternity rather than in a Creator in time. To me, creation is a magnificent condition, without beginning and without end and without the need for a Creator.

The human role

I firmly believe that we human individuals, as creative and conscious participants in the current phase of the evolutionary process, can help restore and maintain coherence in a world which now seems to be degenerating into decay and division.

Our contribution depends on whether, within the world where we live and within ourselves, we can restore the balance between the opposite sides inherent in dualisms, whose unjustified radicalisation in our minds is the reason why the situation has clearly got out of hand in our world today. We often think in terms of radical dualisms because we have lost sight of their inner coherence. It is time we do something about the root cause of the confusion, a confusion which stems from compartmental thinking, with strong partitions between compartments, and black-and-white thinking, leading to a loss of integrity and coherence in society and within ourselves.

I believe that one reason why our functioning on earth has lost its coherence is that our world view has relied too much and too long on material and measurable external phenomena in creation and too little on non-material and non-measurable internal aspects. What is required is no less than a renewed coherence between economy and ecology, female and male, culture and nature, religion and science, between the inside and outside. It is an enormous task which might require a substantial change in our values. But it would allow us to prevent a situation – within the next 25 years in my estimation – where without any policy change our children and grandchildren might discover that they are living on an uninhabitable planet. I suspect that before we have restored our sense of connectedness, a new radical discontinuity will occur.

In making this statement, I am not being pessimistic but realistic. And I'm being optimistic in thinking that, if we seize the opportunities available to restore coherence and equilibrium, then we will be able to turn the tide notwithstanding that we have little time to waste.

Three Windows on Eternity is an account of my findings during a lifelong search to discover the initial intrinsic coherence in the evolutionary process within creation and thus to find a source of inspiration which will restore the coherence in how we experience our existence on earth. I hope that this account will inspire or focus the readers who wonder about their own place and role in this wonderful life on earth.

The story is the result of my own study of secondary sources, the material available in the literature, and my own reflections and opinions. I am not a scientist or philosopher, and I do not pretend to be. But I do try to understand what science has discovered about evolution. In doing so, I have been helped by my educational background as a chemical engineer. As most of us lead busy lives, I have avoided a lengthy script and opted for compact reasoning often leaving out the finer points of the argument. For readers who are interested in the sources – besides my own reflection – from which I have drawn inspiration, knowledge and arguments, I have included a bibliography listing some books published recently as well as some classics.

2
Evolution
An ongoing and relevant process

During my search I gradually became aware of the essence of evolution in creation. And by evolution I mean the entire 13.5-billion-year-old process of evolution, starting with the Big Bang – not limited to biological evolution but encompassing all evolution *prior* to Darwin and *prior* to Genesis.

It became clear to me that the first 10 billion years of inorganic evolution in the universe proceeded according to a strict and coherent pattern. It was a creative process at the level of relatively simple atoms, molecules and planets, without any genes, without any mutations, without chance and without natural selection.

The process started with the Big Bang. Seemingly out of nowhere and without any explanation, a number of *fundamental physical constants of nature* appeared as a one-off event. They became decisive factors in the future course of evolution in creation. For me, this discontinuity is the first major mystery in creation.

At the end of the 10 billion years, or roughly speaking 3.5 billion years ago, life on earth suddenly emerged as a one-time event, without anyone being able to determine where, when and how it emerged. We may understand the chemistry and physics of life processes, but we have never seen 'new life' emerge in nature or in any laboratory. Life can only come from life. I see the one-off emergence of life as the second major mystery in creation.

In the 3.5 billion years following the emergence of life, we see a process of organic evolution that is less strict but still coherent. Through trial and error, it has led to more and more complex and vulnerable organisms, an increasing degree of consciousness and a more intensive interaction with the environment. At first, we see mutations and chance but then direction and natural selection as well. We can still see the outlines of a pattern but with more degrees of freedom for the participants in the process.

This phase in evolution, where we human beings now exist as influential participants, was the subject of Darwin's theory on the origin of species. His theory is not about evolution *before* the emergence of life, nor the emergence of life itself. It is about evolution *after* the emergence of life. It is about biology.

We then have the third, one-time, major mystery, namely the emergence of self-reflective consciousness in *Homo sapiens* approximately 200,000 years ago. In the last few thousand years, this has led to a very rapid spiritual, immaterial evolution of human knowledge and creativity, both qualitatively and quantitatively. At the same time, through the explosive development of communication methods, it has led to a collective consciousness in mankind that extends globally. This new evolutionary phase – following the inorganic and organic stages – can be termed 'cultural' or 'spiritual' evolution. It is a new discontinuity, from a material plane of atomic, molecular and cellular configurations to an immaterial plane of spiritual configurations of the mind.

In the past few decades, our enquiry into the mystery of the mind has improved our understanding of how the material, neuronal configuration in the brain operates. However, the link with the mental configuration of our self-reflective consciousness continues to be an inexplicable phenomenon.

Explosive acceleration

The evolutionary phase following the emergence of a self-reflective consciousness – designated by Teilhard de Chardin as the domain of the spiritual *noosphere* and preceded by the inorganic *geosphere* and organic *biosphere* – is progressing at breakneck speed, unhindered by sluggish material, biological and genetic processes of transfer. This superfast evolution of the noosphere is now being stimulated further by the advanced communication and data-processing technologies which have been developed by the individual minds of human beings and the collective mind of mankind, enabling the same access to the most recent information to anyone anywhere on earth at any time. The computer is catching up with the brain: mankind is transcending biological evolution. And concurrently, there has been exponential growth in the world population from about 2 billion to 7 billion in the last one hundred years.

With the accumulation of all these rapidly occurring phenomena in the current evolutionary phase of our planet, we are losing our sense of connectedness even though our interdependence is increasing. If we are to restore and maintain that sense of connectedness, we will have to make an all-out effort.

Intermission

Inspired by Teilhard de Chardin's theory of evolution, which I saw as a new and broad world view, I continued my journey of discovery and, in 1986, arrived at an intermediate station with the book *Tao, Teilhard en Westers Denken* (published in 1992 as *The Transformation Factor*). In this book, I describe the congruence between the views expounded by Teilhard and the views of the 2500-year-old philosophy of Taoism in China. I had become thoroughly acquainted with Taoism through my own study of the subject and conversations with experts during many business trips to Taiwan in the late 1970s and early 1980s.

Further study of Taoist thought between 1980 and 1984 revealed to me that any congruence with Teilhard's thought had not really dawned on him, even though he had worked as a palaeontologist in China for more than 25 years. He regarded Taoist thought as passive and world-denying, and did not go into it any further.

In both cosmologies, there is an intrinsic connectedness between the universe (heaven), earth and man. They both recognise – even if this is not always realised – the connectedness between the seemingly contradictory elements of dualisms which each exists only by the grace of the other, such as light and dark, life and death, hard and soft, material and spiritual, body and soul, inside and outside, creation and evolution, eternity and time, and more as we saw in the previous chapter.

In *The Transformation Factor*, I compare these two philosophies with the western, materialistic lifestyle of society today, which seems to be losing its coherence. The book shares my ideas on how we can apply the insights from the works of Taoism and Teilhard to restore that coherence. In doing so, we might be able to turn the process that is making human society more and more vulnerable.

The computer is catching up with the brain: mankind is transcending biological evolution.

The essential point in my conclusions is that we should shy away from the tendency to pigeonhole the various social, philosophical and scientific disciplines through specialisation and compartmentalisation and from seeing them as separate entities. When compartmental thinking is taken too far, the benefits derived from progress in some areas are outweighed by the drawbacks associated with alienation from the whole. In other words, there is a loss of internal coherence. And coherence is the hallmark of evolution.

Ecology and economy

At that time, I saw a connection between this conclusion and the supposed opposition between ecology and economy in human society in the current phase of evolution. Because the general acceptance of such an opposition – with ecology usually subordinated to economy – threatens the liveability of our planet for future generations, I became involved with the subject in in the mid-1980s and spent considerable time on it in the next twenty-odd years.

I started looking for practical solutions that would unite economy with ecology at the macro level of technology and business in developed countries, at the micro level of communities in developing countries, and sometimes both. In Taiwan, an isolated island, I saw an opportunity to gain concrete and practical experience. In 1986, I initiated a plan for a local study of the effects of 10 per cent economic growth per annum for a 30-year period if no ecological consequences were taken into account. I was convinced that this economic miracle of the Far East was clearly heading for ecological disaster, with the pollution of rivers, air and soil, an impaired biodiversity and poor public health.

In 1989, following three years of work with an interdisciplinary team of western and Taiwanese experts, the conclusion in the report *Matching*

Economic Growth with Environmental Protection was an eye-opener for the political establishment and business community in Taiwan. Shortly thereafter, an Environmental Protection Agency with ministerial powers was created.

On the basis of my experience with this project, I set up the Ecological Management Foundation in 1990 with the aim of helping to restore the connection between ecology and economy – particularly in the world of business.

Other dichotomies

Having by now arrived at the threshold of the 21st century, I gradually shifted my attention from the imbalance between ecology and economy to other relationships underlying and associated with that imbalance, most notably the relationship between the female and male elements in human society. I saw a pattern in the tendency of the male to focus on economy and the female on ecology.

In 2000, I published a book entitled *Over Vrouw en Man, De Onverbrekelijke Samenhang* (published in 2002 as *Closing the Gap*). In this book, I underpin my thesis that the equilibrium between the female and male elements in society has been disrupted during thousands of years of human social evolution, but will be restored in the 21st century.

In the small communities of prehistoric times, it was clear that male and female originally complemented each other and were largely interchangeable in their roles. In subsequent periods, male domination and the associated role models, as well as missed opportunities to mend the partnership, completely upset the balance. I am convinced that in the 21st century we have reached a juncture where, in the western world, a slow but irreversible process has begun to restore the balance. We can see this, for instance, in statistical data showing a sharp rise in the participation of women in organisations across all of society, including management positions. My book states that the degree of participation is unlikely ever to exceed much more than 25 per cent, given the biological differences between women and men. This however is more than enough to reshape organisational cultures and decision-making processes and to foster a balanced view on ecological issues and on gender relations.

As a result of my intensive experience and close involvement with the process of analysing and reconciling the dichotomy between economy and ecology and between the male and female elements in society, I became curious about the origins of the dualistic oppositions in the evolutionary phase we are going through today.

The emphasis on scientific thought in the past few decades has prevented insight into the mysteries in creation.

It took me back to what I experienced as a student in Delft. I came to realise that the oppositions often flow from a separation between the humanities (or arts) and sciences which has crept into western ways of thinking. The arts and sciences are characterised by different modes of thought.

This compartmental thinking has resulted in many new scientific and technological insights, but the emphasis on scientific thought in the past few decades has prevented insight into the mysteries in creation. The intrinsic connectedness between modes of thought in the arts and sciences demands renewed attention.

A new outlook on life

The search for coherence in creation has taught me that, although science has moved forward enormously in explaining the phenomena in creation, the all-encompassing process of evolution is still filled with inexplicable mysteries. In the attempt to shed light, it appears that the traditional approach, proceeding from the measurable and the visible, is starting to reach its limits more and more clearly. For a long time, consciously or otherwise, we have ignored the world outside of what is measurable and visible and this exclusion has been an inviolable axiom of scientific research.

I realised that we live in four worlds, which we often perceive as separate because of our compartmental thinking but which should be experienced as an integral whole as noted above. By these four worlds I mean the *macro world* of the universe, the *micro world* of the atom, the *meso world* of our daily lives, and the *meta world* of non-material reflection and spirituality. These worlds are inextricably present and interconnected in our individual being. For now, the natural sciences – hampered by the dogmatic and compartmental definition of their domain – block any consideration of the meta world. Yet I believe that this world provides the link with the mysteries in creation.

The meta world cannot be explored but can certainly be experienced.

Actually experiencing the interconnectedness of the four worlds myself in the past few decades has inspired me to forge links between much of the compartmental thought and actions I encounter in daily life. And it has put me on the way to a more coherent outlook on life and the world.

The three mysteries and the meta world provide a bridge between time and eternity. The mysteries suggest that there is a limit to our scientific ability to explain phenomena. They offer windows on eternity and access to transcendental and mystical experience, a forbidden fruit in the world of rationality. The meta world suggests that there is a further dimension outside the boundaries of the three worlds we acknowledge. The meta world is a world we experience.

What lies on the other side, beyond those boundaries – at least that is how we compartmentalise the question – is non-measurable, invisible, inconceivable, timeless and spaceless. This is what I perceive as eternity, a notion which cannot be explored but can certainly be experienced. What I experience is a reality, though not a physical reality. It is a metaphysical reality.

My search has made me realise that creation – without origin and without centre – is a condition linked to eternity while evolution is a process linked to time. The paradoxical combination of eternity and time in an evolving creation continues within myself, because as a spiritual being I feel part of creation, and as a physical being I feel part of evolution. This way of seeing things affords peace through the eternal stability in creation and inspiration through the dynamism of evolution.

It has by now become clear to me that creation is founded on a robust and coherent pattern and, at the same time, that the process of evolution is giving its participants more and more creative power. In making these observations, I personally do not believe in a 'Creator'. Such an approach would be too simplistic and anthropocentric. I believe in 'creation', where I participate in a universal process of ongoing transformation, not steered from without, but generated from within. 'My birth and my death are no more than moments in the universal process of transformation,' the Taoist philosopher Lieh Tzu wrote around 300 BC.

What I have discovered and experienced in my search for coherence to me does not quite fit into any of the stories of creation as developed through the centuries from the various philosophical, religious and scientific views of the world. Whether you call it theism, deism, atheism, pantheism, panentheism, humanism, nihilism, gnosticism, agnosticism, Buddhism, Sufism, Hinduism, Shintoism, Taoism, Judaism, Christianity

I do not believe in a 'Creator'. I believe in 'creation'.

or Islam, all of these great and impressive centuries-old views of the world have a deeply rooted story behind them, their own story about creation. But I do not feel entirely comfortable with any one of them except perhaps Taoism. I feel most comfortable with what is for me the new story of evolution – an ongoing process in the past, present and future – where we experience four coherent worlds with the meta world as an inextricable part.

3
The meta world rediscovered

In our everyday lives, we generally stay – and prefer to stay – in what we consider the real world, a world we understand and hold dear. This is what I call the meso world. Why meso? Because it indicates something in-between, between big and small, between the macro and the micro worlds.

The macro world is what I call the infinitely large world of the universe, the majestic and seemingly eternal universe or cosmos. They are names and words for something we cannot describe because ultimately we do not know what it is. The macro world is not equally accessible to everybody. After all, astrophysics, relativity theory and fundamental constants of nature are not everyday topics of conversation in the meso world.

You can feel a connection with the macro world if you lie on your back outside on a clear night and gaze at that magnificent star-spangled sky. Then perhaps it will dawn on you that the macro world of the universe determined the origin of our human existence and that we descend from it. This makes us part of the macro world.

The micro world is what I call the world of that intangible, purely theoretical, subatomic, quantum physics, which we can not or only barely picture. The micro world of quantum theories is an even less light-hearted topic of conversation in the meso world because only a handful of quantum theorists understand in detail what it is about.

Even so, it is not such a bad idea to know something about it given that the whole quantum world is hard at work in our bodies 24 hours a day, in the form of billions of atoms. Would the owner of such a wonderful enterprise not want to know who his workers are and what they do?

And then there is the immaterial meta world. This I experience as a world which together with the material worlds of our existence constitutes an integral whole. This is the world of emotions, artistic experiences, intuition, affectivity, creativity, information and spirituality.

It is very difficult for us to imagine these macro, micro and meta worlds, which are all present within our human existence. The best minds have been poring over and plodding away at the problem to this very day. They have unleashed the most esoteric formulae and impenetrable theories and experiments, but all beyond the grasp of ordinary folk.

So we generally leave the subject alone; life is hard enough as it is. We simply keep busy in the meso world. This is the world we are familiar with, even if it looks different for every individual. That after all depends on how you plan your day, on your business, social and family commitments, your hobbies, travel, sport and shopping, your household finances, parties, your health, and your time-consuming addiction to television, computer games and internet. Our body has only a short life in the meso world, and we spend most of our time living that life as long, as safely, as comfortably, as creatively and as responsibly as possible.

Sometimes you realise that you have a full life but an empty existence. It is full because you are very busy with the pleasures and duties of the day. At the same time, it is empty because you lack a well-considered outlook on life. You lack a coherent view of the world which would give your life a purpose or meaning outside purely materialistic and social comfort but which you do not get around to in your busy meso world.

This is why besides their daily routines people every now and then look for the meaning of life, sometimes in religious belief, sometimes in self-reflection, in meditation or in an intimate exchange of ideas with friends. And the conclusion is usually along the lines of: 'Of course, I believe in "something" but I'm not quite sure what that is. It's complicated and vague so let's just leave it.' A birth, death, serious illness or personal drama usually leads to renewed contemplation, but then it is quickly forgotten or pushed away and it is back to business as usual.

Be that as it may, in my own life, I have on occasion tried to study those 'other' macro, micro and meta worlds, so that I would at least have some idea of what I was missing by living exclusively in the meso world. The ultimate outcome was a revelation. Although I cannot always follow the exact details of many past and recent discoveries about the three worlds, I have still managed to develop a feel for how the four worlds are interconnected.

Rather than constituting four 'different' worlds, they constitute an integral whole if only because I – a living and thinking human being – have those worlds in me. The atoms in my body are the micro world, as are the neurons in my brain. The emotions inherent in my spiritual experiences are the meta world. My inextricable bond with the earth and with the origin of the universe is my connection with the macro world.

I exist concurrently in macro, micro and meta dimensions and, proceeding from those worlds, I live a meso life. Once you realise this, you can explain to yourself quite rationally, and perhaps also feel emotionally (this is more difficult and takes time but is more direct) that everything in the universe is present in man, in other words within yourself, in its entirety. This is what Mencius, a Taoist philosopher, wrote as early as 400 BC: 'All things (in the universe) are complete in us.' When we try to penetrate the various worlds, we are not simply spectators. We do not simply 'look' at them but we are those worlds. So that is very close.

In actual fact, we – you and I – *are* creation. Given this discovery, I believe in creation, to which I belong, and in an evolution in creation, where we, as self-conscious individuals, act as co-creators. Thus, as a spiritual being, I feel connected with creation in eternity and, as a physical being, I feel connected with evolution through time. I do not see a 'Creator' in this line of thought but that is a question of personal interpretation.

Discovering the meta world

My attitude to life derives from a blend of reason and emotion. The intellectual argument about a co-creative role appeals to me and is one that I can put into practice in daily life, where I have ample opportunity and possibility to help create a meaningful society. This is the rational argument associated with evolution. The emotional element is more difficult because the connection with eternity which I experience as a spiritual being is not based on reason. Pascal once said: '*Le coeur a ses raisons que la raison ne connaît point*' ('The heart has its reasons which reason knows nothing of').

So later in life I began to look for what my heart tells me and how that fits in with what my power of reason tells me. Many people do not need to do this at all. But someone who as a youth, in response to the question of whether he believed in anything, did not get beyond a vague 'something' – albeit embedded in the Christian culture of western Europe – and who then spent seven years in the materialistic, mechanistic bastion of a university engineering programme has some catching up to do. Blessed with the longevity needed to spend many years catching up, I benefited from that very same education, which not only taught me to think in practical terms but also made me understand reasonably well how the world of science works. I learnt to speak the language of the logos. But I still had a great deal to learn about the language of the mythos.

And so I arrived at the fourth world, the meta world. There is no well-defined, specialised field of study for this world because the meta world cannot be studied scientifically. Science is concerned with theories, discoveries and inventions which can be verified and falsified by testing them against data from the real world. Falsification means that human interpretations of natural laws always seem to have an inherent limitation which sooner or later will be superseded by the advancement of knowledge. By definition, a scientific theory can never be perfect. A model is not the same as reality. The map of France is not France itself.

But the meta world is a non-material world. It cannot be measured, reproduced or falsified and so, by definition, it cannot be explored scientifically. It is, however, a world which can be experienced. I had often thought about the notion of a meta world but with interruption and varying intensity and always with some shadow of doubt stemming from my upbringing in a down-to-earth, wartime environment and subsequent education in the sciences.

Even though the meta world is not a well-defined concept – at least not in the sciences – it still exists because it is experienced. Meta denotes 'beyond', as in beyond what is material, tangible, and measurable. To scientists, it is a seemingly unmanageable concept although quantum theory has built a first bridge between what is measurable and non-measurable in the micro world with the concept of non-separability, which suggests that everything in the universe outside of our space-time model is interconnected.

So how should we picture that meta world? One way is to see the material world as the world of the visible outside and at the same time to recognise that there is always an invisible inside. This appeals to us as we experience within ourselves that our own visible material outside has an invisible immaterial inside.

A similar approach is to see the outside of things as the measurable, physico- and thermo-energetic sides of reality and the inside as the non-measurable, spiritual, psycho-energetic aspects of reality. In the latter category, I include such things as life energy, affection, compassion, creativity, mysticism and not least information exchange.

We know and feel that the energy on the inside of our lives plays a major role, but we have no relevant formulae. We simply call it psycho-energy. As we will see in Chapter 7, this takes us to the realm of panpsychism and a concept postulated by Strawson, who regards a concrete experience in the immaterial sphere as an *experiential reality*, i.e. as a component of physical reality, not to be confused with the reality of physics, which only represents material forms.

The equations of physics – as well as chemistry and thermodynamics – only refer to the mechanical and caloric energy of the outside, not the creative energy of the inside. By speaking of emergent, self-organising, spontaneous (here I am using the language of the scientific literature) forces or fields in the evolutionary innovations seen in material phenomena, researchers are in fact implicitly assuming that there is information from within which cannot be captured in formulae.

Not just physics

In the natural world surrounding us, too, there are not only physical phenomena and chemical and physical processes, but also non-material phenomena such as life, creativity and affection. And it is these non-measurable factors which are often the source of innovation. What compels an atom to jump to a completely different molecular model without any intermediate steps, and what compels a molecule to jump to an entirely new cellular model? What motivates nature to create a new state in a one-off step? Here, I am talking about that initial moment, not the subsequent mechanisms of replication and repetition, no matter how fascinating and creative they may be.

Non-measurable factors such as life, creativity and affection are often the source of innovation.

The fact that the energy on the inside does not appear in classical and modern sciences is one of the reasons why these sciences can never describe the meta world. As a result, they can never completely describe the holistic interconnectedness of the four worlds. This might be one reason why the technologies invented by humans using non-holistic classical science are often disruptive and alien to the integrity and holistic structure of nature. Put differently, there will be a conflict between integration and specialisation, between nature from the inside and technology from the outside, until the sciences start to incorporate the meta world into their description of reality. Here, there is still a long way to go.

An opening?

In my opinion, the only opening in classical mechanics to the meta world is the notion of *entropy*. Entropy is a concept captured in a mathematical formula which says that, within a closed system, every exchange of energy results in a decrease in the amount of usable energy and in the degree of order in the system. This ultimately leads to a state that is irreversible, uniform, amorphous and lifeless, with the amount of energy at a minimum. Only the supply of energy and information from outside can preserve the amount of usable energy and the degree of order or, in entropy terms, 'maintain a low degree of entropy'. The higher the degree of order, the lower the entropy; conversely, the lower the degree of order, the higher the entropy.

Entropy is something you cannot picture physically but has intrigued me immensely ever since my days as a student in Delft. It was discovered by Carnot in 1825 and is the only concept in the classical natural sciences which contains the element of irreversibility. To illustrate with a simple example: when you mix half a glass of cold water with half a glass of warm water, you get a glass of lukewarm water. Without intervention from outside, you cannot reverse the action to get two half glasses of water at different temperatures. The higher temperature of the half glass of warm water will not return of its own accord and usable energy has been lost. The entropy of the system has increased irreversibly.

What has always struck me is that the law of entropy – also known as the second law of thermodynamics – is assumed to apply as a matter of course in scientific descriptions of processes in the universe as if that universe were a closed system. It is an assumption which has not been scientifically verified or refuted. My own belief is that evolution is linked to time and produces entropy, while creation is linked to eternity and absorbs entropy. The idea of entropy absorption from beyond the universe was postulated as early as 1948 by scientists Fred Hoyle, Thomas Gold and Hermann Bondi in their continuous-creation theory. It is pure speculation but I am drawn to the existence of increasing entropy in evolution and decreasing entropy in creation: a coherence between two opposites each of which complements and exists by the grace of the other – the essence of the Tao.

The view that in due course the universe will slide down into a lifeless, orderless and amorphous state of maximum entropy seems to me an unwarranted extrapolation of a purely mechanistic and material picture of a universe isolated from the meta world. My own perception is that the meta world is one inseparable component of all four worlds taken together, and the immaterial energy and information which may well flow from that world cannot simply be ignored. After all, the energy and information available at the Big Bang came from somewhere beyond the universe. I think that here there is also a link with the non-separability principle of quantum theory, which states that everything within and outside of our space-time model is interconnected. But our familiar world of classical intuition, a limited world in hindsight and inherited from the Enlightenment, has always ignored and blocked any link from the material world to the meta world.

This link can be restored through the notion of the inside and the outside. The idea of the inside of matter – an inside which is invisible to the eye but present everywhere – can be applied to the entire process of cosmic evolution. During this process, the presence of the inside unfolded as consciousness, starting from the very smallest material manifestations, and in humans – the most complex organisms – has evolved into self-reflective consciousness. And this consciousness provides us with a bridge to the non-material world, the meta world.

The noosphere

Teilhard de Chardin believed that, in the course of cosmological evolution, the degree of immaterial consciousness increases along with the complexity of material phenomena. In his view, the evolutionary history of the earth in the past 4.5 billion years has seen consciousness unfold from the inorganic geosphere through the organic biosphere to culminate in the noosphere (from the Greek word *nous* or mind), a non-material dimension which fits in closely with the concept of the meta world. In this noosphere, he saw the emergence of an expanding reservoir of collectively registered factual experiences on the part of the human individual and mankind and, based on this reservoir, a growing collective planetary consciousness – an everlasting medium.

Self-reflective consciousness provides us with a bridge to the non-material world, the meta world.

Teilhard considered the noosphere as an important dynamic element in cosmogenesis, as an environment where the evolutionary process of transformation at the level of the human species could develop very rapidly, thus circumventing the exceedingly slow mechanism of material evolution via cell division, genetic mutation and propagation. For instance, the human eye is very similar to what it was 3000 years ago but, through technological innovation, we can use that same eye to look further into the macro world of the universe and the micro world of the atom than the eye itself will ever be able to. And this ability is passed on directly through the transfer of knowledge. Our natural senses are supplemented with mechanical instruments.

The enormous acceleration in the transformation from natural organisms to intelligent instruments can be found on all fronts of knowledge acquisition. It is leading to fundamental changes, to discontinuities and hence transformations or 'leaps' in the evolution of human society. An apt example is the exponential growth in the capacity of computers to handle complex systems, their ability to invent and perhaps ultimately their creative intelligence, which at the current pace may well have outstripped that of the human brain by 2035. In that event, the noosphere will have surpassed the biosphere. Raymond Kurzweil describes this phenomenon in his book *The Singularity is Near* (see also Figure 07 on p. 109).

If at that time such leaps in the evolution of human society do occur, where will they lead? This is something the atom, the molecule and the cell did not anticipate either before the leap to the organism occurred in the cosmogenetic process.

In his vision of cosmogenesis, Teilhard does not ask any questions about the reasons for the emergence or direction of the universe, life and consciousness, but he was aware of the interconnectedness between the four worlds, including the meta world. And even though his perception of the meta world was coloured by his Christian beliefs, he could not resist the temptation to label the final destination of mankind as the *Omega Point*, where everything is consciousness and nothing is matter. Is this similar to the exponential growth towards the phenomenon of singularity, or the meta world? The future will tell and, I expect, before the middle of the 21st century.

The Tao of meta

The meta world has actually always been the domain of the world's main religions. Taoism too, though not usually called a religion, has assigned a role to the meta world in its doctrine. The Taoist world view maintains that everything in the universe consists of two inextricably linked complementary components: the inside and the outside, body and mind, heaven and earth, female and male, material and immaterial, and so on – the symbolism of Yin and Yang.

This line of thought does not lead to questions about the origin of the universe, the origin of life or the origin of consciousness. In the Taoist world view, everything which exists is a given condition and everything, including the immaterial meta world, is interconnected in eternity. There is no need of a single Creator but of creation stories as well as many gods and goddesses.

Universal coherence is inherent in the Tao, which encompasses and gives rise to all things, to the one and to ten thousand things. It sounds simple enough. But only after having read a dozen or so translations of the *Tao Te Ching*, the *Book of the Way and its Virtue* and the basic document setting out Taoist thought, did I begin to get a feel for the ideas the texts aim to convey.

The *Tao Te Ching* was probably compiled around 500 BC, by Lao Tzu according to legend, in a form of poetry rather obscure to westerners. It is the most authentic work from all the civilisations of that period because a copy dated 300 BC was found in China which is closer to the likely source than the canon of any other civilisation, including the Old Testament. What the ambivalent texts mean becomes crystal clear once you go through them regularly and allow the seemingly illogical yet meaningful texts to merge as you reflect on them. I think it is a majestic piece of work, consisting of 81 verses and each no more than a quarter of a page. It puts you on the right track to the meta world.

Quantum theorist Niels Bohr – as well as quantum scientists today – see a connection between quantum insights such as non-separability and the interchangeability and substitutability of opposites, on the one hand, and the simple principle of the Tao, on the other. The most recent though still embryonic development in computer technology, which no longer employs the binary language of (0) or (1) but a language of (0) and (1) simultaneously using so-called qubits, is producing a mind-boggling increase in processing speed. In 2008, quantum physicist Carlo Beenakker gave a lecture entitled *Magische Technologie (Magic Technology)* on the subject before the *Koninklijke Hollandsche Maatschappij der Wetenschappen* (Royal Dutch Society of Sciences) and referred to the symbolism of the Tao.

With my western background, I can perhaps understand the essence of Taoism but I cannot fully assimilate it. To really experience it, you need to be devoted and practised through and through. But intensive sharing of its rituals, writings and images has sometimes brought me very close to grasping what the meta world means. Such moments can lead to mystical visions.

When you weave mystical experiences into an awareness of the mysteries of the universe, of life and the mind – as described in the present book – then windows open up on the eternity of the meta world. I imagine this is what you will experience when your life is over, and you go literally beyond the material world, to a world where questions about identity, about why, where from, and where to are not relevant. You will go back to the heart of the mysteries, where the four worlds melt together.

In the words of Chuang Tzu, a Taoist philosopher who lived in the 4th century BC: 'In losing selfhood I shall remain what at bottom I always was, identical with everything conscious and unconscious in the universe.' I suspect this was Chuang Tzu's perception of the meta world.

The Tao that can be spoken of is not the Tao itself.

The name that can be given is not the name itself.

The unnameable is the source of the universe.

The nameable is the originator of all things.

Therefore, oftentimes without intention I see the wonder of Tao.

Oftentimes with intention I see its manifestations.

Its wonder and its manifestations are one and the same.

Since their emergence, they have been called by different names.

Their identity is called the mystery.

From mystery to further mystery:

The entry of all wonders!

Chapter 1 of the *Tao Te Ching*

4
Intriguing discontinuities

Whatever your religious views or philosophical convictions, the evolution of the universe, the earth and life is nothing less than majestic. A bird's eye view tells us that there is a very coherent and consistent pattern.

We have mapped the evolutionary process since the beginning of the universe reasonably well as a result of unbelievably clever and detailed research. Our understanding of the complex physical and chemical processes continues to improve, and not only can we follow them but sometimes we can also predict them.

Nevertheless, a few one-off major discontinuities as well as a string of smaller ones which have occurred within the evolutionary process seem to defy scientific explanation. We are left with unresolved questions about the origin of the information which initiated the discontinuities and determined the nature of the processes. We cannot find anywhere the information which must have been required to allow the saltatory emergence of completely new phenomena, models and forms. Nor do the preceding phases in any way seem to build up towards them or indicate that they would occur. At least, we cannot explain them using the scientific models generally accepted in the micro, macro and meso worlds without including the meta world.

It is not a question of missing links or 'gaps' in our knowledge of a gradual process, sometimes explained as divine intervention by the 'God

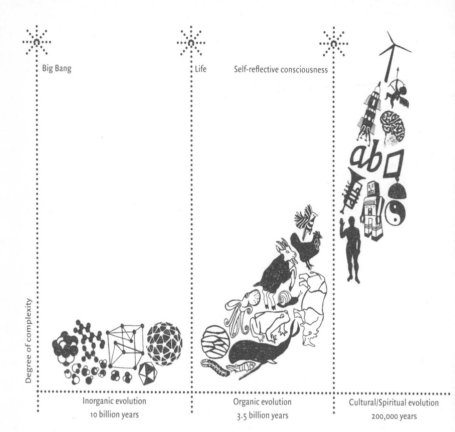

Big Bang

Life Self-reflective consciousness

Degree of complexity

Inorganic evolution
10 billion years

Organic evolution
3.5 billion years

Cultural/Spiritual evolution
200,000 years

01) Complexity over time

of the Gaps', because once these gaps have been filled through advancing scientific research, this God would suddenly no longer be needed. Such an approach is overly simplistic. What we have are saltatory one-off discontinuities, interrupting an otherwise gradual process of growth, which science could not predict.

In the following three chapters, I will describe essentially three key discontinuities, which I call 'major mysteries'. These mysteries have certain common characteristics, namely their sheer uniqueness, their decisive role in the entire process of evolution and their pivotal part in the emergence, existence and future of mankind and human society. I am referring to the mysteries of the emergence of the universe, of life and of self-reflective consciousness, or the mind.

The first 10 billion years of evolution are based on a given condition.

In the periods between the major mysteries, there was a gradual evolution towards new structures, resulting in ever larger and more complex models and forms. The emergence of these forms has always been characterised by an existing model growing larger and larger and eventually reaching the limits of manageable coherence.

This began with the transition from the atomic model to the molecular model, then continued from molecule to cell, from cell to organism and onwards to societies and organisations. With each transition to a new model, the essential nature of the model changed in terms of its internal structure, the forces at play, its coherence, its durability and its interaction with the environment. In actual fact, the emergence of these new models in the intervening periods also involves creative and unpredictable transitions, but they differ in significance from the three major discontinuities referred to above. And they show a recurring pattern so they are not one-off events.

Let me give an example involving the transition from the atomic to the molecular model. With the growth of the atomic model from the smallest atom in nature (hydrogen, with atomic number 1) to the largest atom (plutonium, with atomic number 94), the atomic structure ran into a natural limit beyond which no new forms were stable: larger atoms could still form but in practice often disintegrated immediately. If there was to be further evolutionary growth, then a new model would have to emerge. This manifested itself as a combination of atoms in a new – molecular – structure, more complex in nature and essentially different in terms of configuration and organisation. The emergence of the molecular model after the atomic model was a discontinuous, but logical, next step. And this step was repeated with the formation of every new molecule in the course of evolution.

Everything we have discovered about the course of the first 10 billion years following the major discontinuity of the Big Bang and before the creation of life shows that the evolutionary process from elementary quantum particles up to molecules encompasses a consistent, tightly ordered, refined and dynamic structure, without genes, without chance, and without natural selection. This is why, to me, there cannot be any doubt that the first 10 billion years of evolution are based on a given

The emergence of life was accompanied by the emergence of death.

condition. There was a source of specific information which led to a monumental edifice. When I realised this, it dawned on me that there is more to evolution than the origin of species.

Life on earth

Following the first 9 billion years of cosmic history, the earth was created and 1 billion years later a new evolutionary period began with the emergence of life on earth: the second one-off major discontinuity approximately 3.5 billion years ago.

It seems perfectly logical to me that the principle of a given pattern for the first 10 billion years did not suddenly cease to apply in the next period. And this is borne out by the tightly organised new models emerging in the transition from inanimate molecules to animate cells and then organisms. Each model demonstrates a completely new form of organisation and different binding forces. Complexity increases, leading to more fragile structures, which are increasingly finite in material existence.

While hydrogen atoms, originating more than 13 billion years ago, are virtually indestructible – as is also true for the 12-billion-year-old water molecule – and still exist to this very day, the increasingly complex individual organisms dating from the last 500 million years of evolution generally have only a relatively short lifespan. Not only do the organisms die out but, eventually, so do their species.

From the emergence of life 3.5 billion years ago, single-celled forms – first the prokaryotes (non-nucleated cells) and later the eukaryotes (nucleated cells) – dominated the next 3 billion years of 'eternal' life on earth, without much evolution. Not until an 'explosion' of multi-cellular organisms around 500 million years ago did plants and animals emerge, increasingly complex, increasingly vulnerable and increasingly transient.

The emergence of life was thus accompanied by the emergence of death. With the growing number of variables, and the enormous complexity and fragility of new structures in the process of evolution, there seems to be a greater vulnerability so that new forms of life display shorter and shorter periods of stability. But, at the same time and probably as a consequence, they possess dynamically evolving innovations resulting from their interaction with and adaptation to the environment. This appears to proceed via mutation, random chance and natural selection, with a certain degree of unpredictability and a certain freedom of choice. Now we are getting close to the world of Darwin.

There is not only evolution in creation but also creation in evolution.

This extremely innovative evolutionary period, continuing to this very day, not only builds on a tightly ordered pattern from the previous period, but also reveals a less predictable, unexpectedly new, creative evolution. While cells and organisms ultimately consist of complex structures of old atoms and molecules – themselves the outcome of a pattern in the preceding phase – with the new evolutionary period we have arrived in a process where the living world 'creates' new forms of life. Now, there is not only evolution in creation but also creation in evolution.

Self-reflective consciousness

The third major and one-off discontinuity, namely the emergence of a self-reflective consciousness or the mind, which appeared in humanity about 3.5 billion years after the emergence of life, is more difficult to examine with scientific methods. Although there is a presumption that this 'spiritual' discontinuity arises from the material world, such a position cannot be proved.

Self-consciousness, the psyche, spirit, soul, inspiration, creativity, mind, or whatever you might want to call it, all seem to belong to a non-material world which we are not familiar with and cannot measure but which we do experience. Experiencing the non-material world is a reality as much as exploring the material world is a reality. In this reality therefore lies the link between experience and exploration.

One unresolved issue is how the non-material world we experience communicates with the material world of our brain. Through research into the brain, neurologists, biochemists, psychologists and psychiatrists have made discoveries which have proved successful in curing disease resulting from flaws in or damage to the brain. But we have yet to answer questions about the origin of the information transmitted to neurons, the nature of the transfer mechanism and the exact process governing the two-way interaction between the immaterial mind and the material brain.

Keep looking

Despite our much greater and still growing knowledge of and insight into the processes of evolution, we are still left with mysteries suggesting that there are boundaries to what scientific research into the outside of things can explain.

Research into the processes in the periods following the birth of the universe and following the emergence of life has taught us a great deal about the questions of *what* the processes entail and *how* they function. Research into *why* and *when* the universe, life and self-reflective consciousness emerged, on the other hand, has delivered far fewer results. There is no answer to the pressing question of where we can find the information needed to explain that emergence.

There is great interest in the three major mysteries, as is apparent from the very costly, globally coordinated research programmes which have taken place on all three fronts in the last two decades and continue to take place with the aim of clearing up the mysteries. The last notion is my personal opinion and is not explicitly stated in the programme objectives, but I think it is certainly an important motivator.

The origin of the universe, the Big Bang, is the subject of investigation of the Large Hadron Collider project in Geneva, which became operational in 2010. Hadron, familiar to us as the world's most powerful particle accelerator, is the umbrella term for subatomic particles. The aim of the LHC is to discover an unknown but predicted smallest quantum particle. The existence of this particle should be the final piece in the puzzle of the origin of the universe: an answer to the question of why particles have mass. I will return to this in the next chapter. The LHC project costs €9 billion and will run for many years. Elsewhere, there are already initial plans for an even more powerful particle accelerator.

Then there is the multinational Human Genome project, which aimed to decipher the essential nature of genes and hence the secret of life. The project took 13 years, cost US$3 billion and was completed in 2003. The project has not been able to explain the essence and origin of genes or how they get their information. Nor has it clarified how the chemistry and physics of molecules use genetic 'codes' – a kind of language – to transfer the information needed to maintain life and design organisms. We have only been able to determine that the molecules are an intermediary. We know their composition and have named them, but how the transfer of information proceeds continues to be a mystery. What the Human Genome research has in fact shown is the need for a partial farewell to the purely materialistic approach to biological evolution which stems from the Enlightenment and was promoted by Darwin.

The research showed that our consciousness does not have a material origin in our brain.

One of the principal leaders of the project, the American chemist and biologist Francis Collins – who was a firm atheist long before the start of the project and later quietly converted to Christianity – wrote a book entitled *The Language of God* after the results of the research had been published. He concludes that the emergence of life, the origin of genes and the existence and processing of genetic codes are mysteries which we human beings cannot explain, unlike – as he sees it – the existence of a Creator.

Finally, we have the Decade of the Brain project, whose main goal was to map the entire nervous system of the brain in order to find a cure for neurological diseases and disorders. A secondary objective was to discover the secret of how the brain and mind interact. The project was financed by the United States, the United Kingdom and Japan but I do not have any cost figures. It was completed in 2000. A wealth of knowledge and information was accumulated to achieve the first objective. In addition, the research showed that our consciousness, our mind, does not have a material origin in our brain – a view put forward with increasing force in the previous few decades – but that it must have its own independent and immaterial basis, sending information to the material neural circuits in the brain. In other words, it is the other way round. Exactly how this works continues to puzzle us.

In May 2011, the European Union selected a new initiative for its Future Emerging Technologies (FET) flagship programme, namely the Human Brain project. The aim of the project is to obtain a better understanding of the workings of the brain by means of computer simulation. Nine European universities will execute the programme through various disciplines such as the neurosciences, genetics, applied mathematics, robotics and social sciences.

The international projects outlined above bear testimony to the great significance which political institutions and society attach to unravelling

Our search for the truth has led us to the limits of what we can measure and understand.

the underlying three major mysteries. These efforts have not yet delivered the answers we have been waiting for. To the contrary: two of the programmes, namely the Human Genome and Decade of the Brain projects, have actually confirmed the mysteries. I suspect that the LHC research into the origin of the universe currently underway in Geneva and the EU programme on the human brain will not solve the mysteries either.

The inside and outside

So far, scientists have deliberately and expressly been concerned with just the outside – i.e. the visible, the measurable, the observable, the material phenomena in creation. The Enlightenment led to the expectation that we had almost reached the end of what there was to learn about the design of the universe and that we would ultimately also discover the secret of creation. And then we would no longer expect anything new.

Research into the outside has taught us many things, in particular how we can take better care of our material well-being, how we can defend ourselves against disease and mental and physical harm, as well as how we can better protect nature and hence ourselves. This is an unexpected gift. In the process, and whether we like it or not, the 21st century has seen us come closer and closer to the invisible, to the interface between the material outside and the immaterial inside, and we are reaching out to the 'other side', to the 'beyond', the non-material and non-measurable. Our search for the truth has led us to the limits of reductionist measurement and rational understanding. It is, however, not a final destination but a point of departure. We now encounter the meta world – until very recently forbidden terrain and still a taboo for many 'old-school' scientists.

To these scientists, including some brilliant minds such as Stephen Hawking and Paul Davies, philosophical discussions about the meta world are not relevant. They assume that the physical and mathematical laws of the universe are a given. The resulting fundamental constants of nature give rise to everything that has appeared since the Big Bang. However, these constants of nature assume that the initial state is known. And this continues to be the missing link.

Another missing element is an explanation for the fact that the laws of relativity theory in the macro world cannot be reconciled with the laws of quantum theory in the micro world. Gravity, an important component of relativity theory, does not actually appear in the formulae of quantum theory. An all-encompassing theory known as superstring or M-theory is supposed to solve this, a subject I will return to below.

The deeper origin of the universe, of life and of self-reflective consciousness must lie 'elsewhere'.

But nobody is looking for the origin of the natural constants. When Emperor Napoleon asked French mathematician and astronomer Laplace at the beginning of the 19th century whether there was a role for God in his scientific views on the universe, Laplace is reported to have said: 'I have no need of that hypothesis.' Two hundred years later, Hawking basically says the same thing. But that is not the end of the matter for me. The deeper origin of the universe, of life and of self-reflective consciousness, or the mind, and thus our own origin must lie 'elsewhere'.

So is this where we find the link with the meta world and with eternity? You cannot investigate this indefinable condition; you can only experience it and this is only possible if you stop looking for a rational solution. Then you will discover your own connectedness with that 'other place' and you wander into the realms of mysticism, drawn by the aspect of an unfamiliar eternity. And that is when you open the windows onto the meta world, and throw off the shackles of the limited micro, macro and meso worlds.

There was an awareness of a link with eternity, mystery and mysticism several thousand years ago in every part of the world by all the major philosophical and religious movements. So after 300 years of intellectual and technological voyages of discovery since the Enlightenment, we are back to square one. The meta world is still that very same indescribable world of the inside.

Windows on eternity

I have felt a close attachment to the three major mysteries ever since they dawned on me. To me, they are three windows which look out onto an ineffable eternity where the four worlds melt together into a state that is beyond words, close to the notion of the Tao which, according to the first chapter of the *Tao Te Ching*, is no longer the Tao once you start describing it. So I do not think I can describe an inner experience of ineffable eternity.

What I can describe to some extent is my own path towards such an experience.

5
The universe
A mysterious given

Anyone who has ever stood still to admire the starry sky has undoubtedly wondered how far it extends into the deep recesses of the universe. How did I get here and why? Before I was born, I was nothing. Will I be nothing again after I die?

We actually know nothing about the nature of the origin of the universe or the cosmos. We have two concrete terms for this state, making us think we know what we are talking about. But apparently this is not the case.

There is the theory of the Big Bang, which addresses the observable cosmological process of evolution after the emergence of the universe. As for the point of origin itself, however, and what existed before that point, we are literally groping in the dark. We know that the visible universe is expanding and, on the basis of that expansion, astronomers have calculated back to a point of zero volume when the universe might have emerged. They arrived at 13.7 billion years ago. The calculations are not completely reliable given the recent discovery that the universe has been expanding at a faster rate in the past 5 billion years. Let's just say that the posited primordial explosion took place an awfully long time ago. To keep it simple, I will make it 13.5 billion years.

Our methods to determine the moment when the universe emerged only get us to the moment just after emergence so not quite to the actual moment itself. In professional circles, this barrier is known as *Planck's wall*, after the quantum physicist Max Planck. Here we are dealing with the smallest measures of distance and time that we can still cope with and they are in the order of magnitude of 10^{-35} metres and 10^{-43} seconds. Emergence in terms of space and time at a zero point cannot be measured more accurately with the techniques available. We never quite get to that zero point but get stuck just before it. It is therefore impossible to get a true picture of the origin of the universe. We can derive the beginning as accurately as we can by calculating back from present to past but that is as far as it goes.

Whatever was happening in space and time before the Big Bang – assuming we can still speak of space and time at all – thus remains a mystery. The mystery is all the more intriguing because, in the first nanofraction of space and time, the initial conditions were present for the emergence during the evolution of the universe of all the phenomena we know today: atoms, molecules, stars, the earth, life, man and his consciousness.

Scientists have made exact calculations of the initial conditions immediately after the Big Bang and these appear to be present and unaltered throughout the whole visible universe. The eight key numbers resulting from these calculations are known as the fundamental physical constants of nature. They include the speed of light (c), the elementary charge of an electron (e), Planck's constant (h) and the gravitational constant (G). For the origin of the natural constants, science has come up with the ambiguous concept of 'quantum vacuum', but what's in a name?

Physicists and chemists describe the measurable manifestations in the first nanoseconds of the primordial energy explosion following the mysterious emergence of the natural constants. Here you find the origin of the quantum conditions through which we explore the micro world today. It is not what occupied the pioneering scientists in the 17th century, but we now know that the micro world after the Big Bang constituted the origin of the macro world which emerged later in the evolutionary process. This means an inextricable link, a connectedness, between the micro world and the macro world.

The knowledge of such a link makes it intriguing that we cannot make scientific models of the micro world (quantum theory) fit in with models of the macro world (relativity theory): the four known fundamental forces – the gravitational force or gravity, and the electrodynamic, weak nuclear, and strong nuclear forces – do not all appear in both theories. Specifically, the gravitational force does not appear in the quantum model.

It is a dilemma which Einstein was not able to solve either. Stephen Hawking, the most gifted contemporary theoretical physicist, is determined to find an overall model of the universe encompassing both theories. He believes that *superstring theory*, also known as *M-theory*, is the solution, but acknowledges that we will never know the ultimate initial conditions prevailing *before* the Big Bang. In M-theory, where M stands for 'Mother of all theories' and which is beyond my comprehension, there are ten rather than four dimensions and there is a multiverse of 10 to the power of 500 different universes.

Hawking does assume a design, as is apparent from his book *The Grand Design*, published in 2010. But like Laplace, he does not need a designer. Hawking is not looking for the reason why there are natural constants or the reason why the universe has a particular physical configuration. He takes these as a necessary given, and he wants to produce a complete and coherent picture of the consequences of that given. He hypothesises that something could have spontaneously come from nothing – from the given constants of nature and from gravity in particular. He writes: 'Spontaneous creation is the reason there is something rather than nothing, why the universe exists, why we exist.' In saying so, he is less modest than Isaac Newton, who discovered gravity in the 17th century and wrote: 'Gravity explains the motions of the planets, but it cannot explain who set the planets in motion.' Newton was a religious man.

The notion that the natural constants appear to have sprung from nothing at a single moment remains an undiscussed mystery.

Inorganic evolution

In the cosmological process of evolution following the emergence of the fundamental constants of nature and the subatomic micro world, the macro world began to take shape through the emergence of elements, starting with the first, simplest and lightest element, namely the hydrogen atom. From and after this atom, ever-larger and heavier atoms emerged, chronologically and sequentially, ultimately leading to the 94 elements which now appear in nature.

The first atoms or elements which emerged after hydrogen were, successively, helium, carbon, oxygen, neon, iron, nitrogen, silicon,

The water molecule originated as one of the first molecules in the universe, approximately 12 billion years ago.

magnesium, phosphorus, calcium and sulphur, which today constitute more than 99 per cent of the elements in the visible cosmos. With the exception of helium and neon, these elements are also the ten most important building blocks of the living organisms which emerged on earth billions of years later.

At school we learnt that the elements fit without fail into an ingenious and perfect system, put together and presented as the periodic table of elements by Dmitri Mendeleev in 1869. At school however we did not learn that this collection of elements is not a static and one-off phenomenon, but that the elements must have emerged one after the other from a given initial condition in the course of the first phase of evolution, and that we have no idea how the information needed for the construction and emergence of the elements was passed along and where the information came from.

The predictability of their existence became apparent when Mendeleev found many gaps while constructing the table where elements would fit but had not been discovered. In his day, only 60 of the 94 elements were known. Although in hindsight it transpired that the periodic table was not entirely correct, the prediction of the 34 elements discovered later is rather impressive.

Elements, or atoms, are relatively simple structures, consisting largely of three basic building blocks, namely protons, electrons and neutrons. Only the first atom, hydrogen, lacks neutrons. These three building blocks are present throughout the whole universe, numbering trillions and trillions, and are all identical. But when they combine in threesomes, with equal numbers of protons and electrons and sometimes an equal number of neutrons, they exhibit largely unpredictable, very specific and distinct properties: the properties of the 94 different atoms appearing in nature.

The periodic table ranks them according to atomic number, which gives the number of protons in the nucleus of the atom. For instance, 1 proton and 1 electron form the hydrogen atom (atomic number 1), which – as noted above – is the only atom without any neutrons as its third building block. This element is an odourless and colourless gas with a large number of very specific chemical and physical properties. When 8 protons, 8 electrons and 8 neutrons combine, they create oxygen (atomic number 8), a colourless gas and essential for the existence of life. When 12 protons, 12 electrons and 12 neutrons combine, they form carbon (atomic number 12), a dark solid substance again with its own specific properties and again essential for living organisms. When 29 protons, 29 electrons and 35 neutrons combine, they form copper (atomic number 29), a

Those water molecules originating 12 billion years ago – they make up 70% of the human body.

shiny metal with a red lustre. When 82 protons, 82 electrons and 120 neutrons combine, they form lead (atomic number 82), a heavy, soft, grey-coloured metal. And so it goes on for all of the 94 elements, composed of three building blocks and together displaying a wide variety of totally different specific properties.

During or after the formation of the elements, the first combinations of elements emerged as molecules. Examples are the combination of the oxygen element with the carbon element to form the carbon dioxide molecule, and the combination of oxygen with hydrogen to form the water molecule.

It is worth noting that the water molecule originated as one of the first molecules in the universe, approximately 12 billion years ago, when conditions in the universe – such as temperature, pressure and force fields – were optimal for its formation. The very same water formed at that time can now be found everywhere in the cosmos, including our own earth. That water was of fundamental importance to the emergence of life on earth approximately 8.5 billion years later. Indeed, 70 per cent of the human body consists of water molecules originating 12 billion years ago. For many years, this is something I had never quite realised.

Properties

An intriguing question is how we can explain the forms, shapes, colours, smells and all the other properties of the elementary atoms which appeared in the evolution of this first 10-billion-year phase. The question is equally fascinating at the molecular level, where atoms combine into molecules, minerals, plants and animals. The millions of different molecules all have their own specific properties such as form, shape, colour, consistency and smell.

I will give an example. The element sodium (atomic number 11) is an extremely reactive, grey mass. The element chlorine (atomic number 17) is a green, toxic gas. But – and this is spectacular – when you combine these two atoms to form the molecule NaCl, it turns out to be a harmless edible white substance, namely salt. The form, colour, consistency and the many properties of this compound can on the whole not be predicted from its constituent atoms.

The same intriguing question applies to minerals, plants and animals, which are all made up of molecules and will be covered in the next chapter. From the quantum world, we know the formulae as well as the chemical and physical configuration of observed phenomena to the very smallest micro detail and given such information we can predict a few basic properties. This subject is addressed in such disciplines as developmental biology, fractal theory and quantum mechanics, resulting in what are known as the *laws of form*. Some fascinating discoveries have been made about the way in which mathematico-physical constraints determine the basic forms found in nature. It is possible, for example, to predict whether an element or molecule is a gas, liquid or solid, what its chemical valence is, as well as its conductivity and X-radiation. And yet we do not know the reasons for the very specific exterior forms and countless other properties in which they manifest themselves.

On this point, mechanistic diehards are unyielding, and maintain that all exterior forms and properties can be derived from the atomic and molecular quantum structure. Even if that were partly possible, I am convinced that if a chemical physicist who has never seen sodium in its physical form but who has studied its atomic quantum structure were asked to predict what sodium looks like physically and the dozens of properties it has, he would not be able to do so.

Another striking example of this lack of predictability is the simple water molecule. It displays 62 'anomalies' which can only partly be predicted from its molecular quantum structure. A practical instance of this observation is that water expands when it cools down to minus 4 degrees Celsius before it changes to ice, so that ice is lighter than water and stays floating on top while the temperature of the water underneath remains above 0 degrees. Water can also absorb more heat per unit volume than any other liquid so that our body temperature does not vary excessively.

When I first encountered such phenomena together with the changes in form and colour produced by reactions between chemical substances, at my grammar school in 1943, I knew that I wanted to study chemistry.

A coherent pattern

The majestic process giving rise to the elements, molecules and celestial bodies in the first 10 billion years of the universe has now been completely mapped by modern science. It is baffling in terms of size, structure and order, and the process unmistakably fits into a consistent and coherent pattern, a pattern which must have been inherent in the natural constants of the first nanoseconds after the birth of the universe. The periodic table, too, must have been captured in the natural constants at that time.

'Somewhere' there was a source of information to ensure that the evolution of the universe – a gigantic process in terms of time and scale – would follow a certain arrangement. We are able to understand that arrangement, explain the processes involved and discover patterns. But we do not know what gave rise to the material phenomena we observe, how the information needed for their emergence was transferred or where it came from. The whole edifice seems to have arisen in those first 10 billion years without natural selection, without chance, without the fall of man and without sex. It seems to have arisen in a cosmogenetic process of creation and evolution without the story of the Bible and without Darwin's theory.

We have been extremely clever to have discovered and mapped almost every process, mechanism, and force field in the evolution of the cosmos, to have formulated their interconnectedness mathematically, not to mention many more intellectual feats. But ultimately, we know nothing about the source of the information underlying the laws, systems and discontinuities we observe and chart. The earliest and only information we have about any origin consists of the natural constants which appear to have been present all of a sudden, where there was nothing before, one billionth of a second following the Big Bang. And these constants carried the initial pattern.

Just keep looking?

But meanwhile the journey of discovery continues. In order to penetrate as closely as possible to the origin of the universe, the Hadron particle accelerator in Geneva went ahead in 2010. The objective is to cause protons to collide 800 million times per second at the fastest speed ever and from that collision to create the smallest conceivable particles measuring a trillionth of a millimetre, emitting energy rays lasting one trillionth of a trillionth of a second. To achieve this, a magnetic field is generated which is 100,000 times as strong as that of the earth. The mission of the project, on which more than 7000 quantum physicists are collaborating, is to replicate the conditions at the moment of the Big Bang. The idea is to find new particles, or bosons, which are essential to proving the most recent theories in particle physics – including the superstring theory referred to earlier – and answering the question of why a particle has mass. This would make it possible to formulate the desired all-encompassing model of the universe. The particle in question is called the Higgs particle, after the contemporary Cambridge physicist Peter Higgs, who has predicted their existence. In the language of journalism, the particle is also known as 'the God particle'.

As one of the collaborating physicists put it: 'We don't simulate the conditions of the beginning of the universe; we recreate the conditions.' In July 2012, it was announced that test results had confirmed the existence of the particle. My personal expectation, as a layman, is that the essence of the origin of the Big Bang will remain a mystery.

A foot in the door

A possible opening extending from quantum theory to this mystery is the discovery that when particles (subatomic particles such as photons, protons and electrons) are split into two from an initial two-particle state, they are then able to exchange information simultaneously everywhere in the universe and to retain an inverse symmetry if the 'spin' orientation of one of the particles changes. The transfer of this information is instantaneous and independent of the speed of light, conflicting with Einstein's law that nothing in the universe can move faster than light. In this new line of thought, there exists a spaceless and timeless dimension in the universe. The phenomenon is known as the *non-separability* or *non-locality principle* and also as *entanglement*. It concerns the boundary between the immaterial and material worlds.

This perplexing theory is too complicated to address here. It was corroborated experimentally by the physicist Alain Aspect at the Orsay laboratories in Paris in 1982 and more recently by Nicolas Gisin at the research centre of the University of Geneva. The phenomenon was proved empirically over

We don't simulate the conditions of the beginning of the universe; we recreate the conditions.

small and large distances, without any kind of spatial transfer and without a time path and so without any dependence on location. Hence the term 'non-locality'. In which indefinable medium the connection between the two particles is maintained, we do not know. The meta world?

Einstein disputed the possibility of non-separability in a thought experiment with his colleagues known as the EPR (Einstein, Podolsky, Rosen) paradox. Einstein maintained a mechanistic view of the world where everything can ultimately be defined materially and mathematically. This did not fit in with the new view put forward by quantum theory, where nothing can be determined precisely and where probability calculations and the choice of measurement technique influence the outcome. Einstein responded with his celebrated statement 'God does not play dice', so theist after all for just a moment. Regrettably, he did not live long enough to see the phenomenon of non-separability empirically proved in 1982 and again subsequently. There was also some commotion in 2011 over the hypothesis that nothing can travel faster than light when a CERN study showed that neutrinos appeared to be moving faster than light. But a single study is insufficient evidence.

The EPR paradox and the non-separability argument are unfortunately so difficult to grasp that their significance is not getting through to the general public. I will not go into the technical details any further because it falls outside the scope of my story. I only mention the subject because I feel that the evidence supporting non-separability is a phenomenal breakthrough in the quest to discover how the universe functions, a break from classical intuition where the concepts of space and time are essential.

If everything in evolution emerges through subdivision in space and time, starting from a well-defined (or undefined) moment, then non-separability could apply to everything in the universe, including human experience. Within the atoms in our own bodies, we harbour our own quantum world and thus the phenomenon of non-separability. Since we

Within the atoms in our own bodies, we harbour our own quantum world. all come from one and the same source, we could have access to and a connection with a spaceless and timeless dimension as well as with other people. You might be open to such access under certain conditions, during meditation for instance. You might experience a connection with someone else by 'plucking the right strings'. The connection is like the access via your transistor radio to a cantata by Bach, seemingly from nowhere, simply by finding the right wavelength (vibration). But whereas the radio relies on electromagnetic fields, we have no idea what the medium behind non-separability looks like.

Feet on the ground

As yet all scientific explorations of the cosmos, nature and man almost exclusively pertain to material processes, to order and systems, and to mathematical, chemical and physical formulations and numbers. The question of whether there is an immaterial dimension is hardly ever discussed.

The pioneers of science in the 17th century looked to the Divine for the answer. This was the reason why, for example, they called the golden section the *sectio divina* – a phenomenon, appearing throughout nature, of a fixed ratio between dimensions in natural forms which cannot be expressed as a number from any conventional system of measurement. The same is true for pi, the fixed proportion of the radius to the circumference for any arbitrary circle. These kinds of natural ratios, some of which are referred to as 'transcendental', were at that time regarded as divine signals. Later, with the Enlightenment, religion was renounced as a partner in the search for truth and the models formulated to capture the structure of creation became more and more materialistic, mechanistic, mathematical and compartmentalised. Today, modern scientists explain numbers such as the golden section and pi as a logical consequence of how the cosmos functions, based on the fundamental constants of nature and the laws of form referred to earlier. No mysticism, no mystery, but logic. The question of how those natural constants and laws emerged from nothing is left unanswered and is dismissed as irrelevant.

With much hesitation, given the contamination of the concept of *intelligent design* in dogmatic discussions, some religious, seasoned quantum theorists call these numbers signs of a divine design. This I have experienced in personal conversations.

Whatever you call the mystery of the origin of the universe, we are still left with the riddle of where the concrete information which led to the Big Bang came from – from 'beyond' the universe, from eternity? Who or what (figuratively speaking) governs there is

With the Enlightenment, religion was renounced as a partner in the search for truth.

an unanswerable question. If you are open to mystical experience, then you can look through a window on eternity, leading from mystery to mysticism. For pure materialists, this is an almost unthinkable concession. But when the materialistic-mechanistic view of the world is clearly reaching its limits – something we see happening today as I am trying to show in this book – then the step to the transcendental seems logical.

The notion that the natural constants generated the conditions necessary for a world which also gave rise to the human phenomenon – the most complex organism on earth – has resulted in the assumption that this emergence in our universe was the intention from the very outset, the so-called *anthropic principle*. In other words, the natural constants are supposedly fine-tuned to the emergence of human life. This seems hard to believe.

The unproven M-theory referred to earlier gives a different explanation. According to this theory, there is an incredibly large number of universes, and just as many different combinations of natural constants, which might include a combination whose structure happens to be conducive to the emergence of life and humans. This hypothesis cannot be proved or falsified and is therefore not scientific by definition. Like the notion of a quantum vacuum, the concept of a multiverse is a conjecture that is just as mystical as other unprovable concepts.

All ideas and paradigms concerning the non-measurable world will remain speculative. In the measurable world, too, models continue to be perceptions of a reality, but not the full reality because new models appear to emerge in our brain all the time. We will keep exploring the horizon by putting forward alternative views. We have no idea of how, where and whether the universe is limited in space and time. We cannot imagine a centre of the universe – it seems limitless, infinite, giving a feeling of eternity, of the meta world.

Although Einstein in his relativity theory mathematically formulated the relativity of mass and energy and of space and time, questions about the nature of the source of these relationships remain unanswered. Einstein was a pantheist. In other words, he believed in an omnipresent creation, without beginning, without end and without centre.

What is fascinating about the idea of a universe without a centre is that every place in the universe is then a centre. Having discovered that the centre of the unlimited universe is not the earth, not the sun, not the Milky Way, nor any galaxy, we must conclude that the centre is everywhere. So in myself as well. The observation that I, in my spot on earth, am a centre of the universe comes as quite a revelation.

Intelligent design?

In the preceding material, I have indicated several times that in the construction of atoms and molecules – during the inorganic period of evolution – I firmly believe in the existence of a given pattern. This is a sensitive subject because the western world has now entered into a heated discussion about intelligent design, about whether or not there is a design and a designer. The use of the word 'intelligent' comes from a work by Thomas Aquinas and I feel that the current discussion is applying it too anthropocentrically.

The two sides in the discussion are evolutionists and creationists. The former believe exclusively in Darwin's theory of evolution, based on mutation, chance and natural selection. The latter believe exclusively in a personal Creator, who created all that exists separately and man in particular. These views are considered to be two opposite extremes, an example of the simplistic radicalisation of differences which, in essence, are complementary rather than opposing positions.

The discussion is primarily about evolution or creation after the emergence of the earth and of life, approximately 4.5 and 3.5 billion years ago respectively. The debate is about organic evolution and not about the initial and much longer-lasting inorganic evolution since the Big Bang. The debate is about whether the biological, organic world was created or whether it evolved. It is about the origin of nature and species, including the human race.

However, I think that, prior to any debate about organic evolution, we should first look more closely at evolution and creation in the preceding phase, namely the period of inorganic evolution occupying the first 10 billion years following the emergence of the universe. Then we will not be hampered by any questions about the origin of life, or self-reflective consciousness and about mutation or natural selection since these phenomena did not yet exist.

I myself have no doubt about the existence of a consistent and dynamic pattern in the first 10 billion years of cosmological evolution, a pattern that is robust, coherent, evolution-oriented yet mysterious. From this perspective, the discussion about intelligent design in the subsequent 3.5 billion years changes entirely because biological evolution proceeds from atoms, molecules and minerals which emerged earlier and according to that pattern. It should be clear that, in the process of creation and evolution I have outlined, there is no place for the creationist view or intelligent design.

After the emergence of life, new and innovative elements arise during the period of organic, biological evolution, adding different dimensions. Things are literally livening up.

6
Life
A mysterious phenomenon

When billions of elements, molecules and galaxies were roaming around the universe about 4.5 billion years ago, our solar system and our planet earth were born. We now know fairly accurately from research into the subject how, since that time, physical and chemical processes on earth have led to more and more and increasingly complex manifestations of molecules, cells and organisms.

First there were inorganic molecules, the components of minerals and crystals. Then there were organic molecules, the building blocks first of unicellular and then of multicellular organisms, which ultimately resulted in the millions of earthly species we are familiar with – a hugely diverse collection of forms, shapes, colours, smells and behaviours. Around 3.5 billion years ago, life emerged, judging by fossils found in Western Australia dating back to that time. The emergence of life in that evolutionary phase was a major discontinuity, similar to the mysterious leap at the emergence of the universe.

Mysterious molecules
A fundamental characteristic of the phenomenon of life is self-replicability. Research has shown which molecules are essential to the basic building

blocks of self-replicating systems. We have also worked out whether and where in the past these chemical compounds appeared on earth and even elsewhere in the universe.

Why only these 20 amino acids are suitable for creating living cells is a puzzle.

The key lies in exactly 20 specific amino acids which can be found in nature. Why only these 20 amino acids are suitable for creating living cells is a puzzle. Chemists have been able to create 60 other synthetic amino acids which also exist in nature or could have existed. Nevertheless, all living creatures on earth consist of just those 20 amino acids. This is true for bacteria, plants, insects, fish, reptiles, birds, mammals and human beings.

Another puzzle is that the 20 amino acids are almost exclusively of the 'left-handed' variety. A note of explanation is required here. Many organic molecules have the property that they appear in two configurations whose chemical composition is identical. But some of the atoms in the molecule may have opposite optical orientations. This orientation is measured by allowing polarised light to pass through the molecules. The light bends to the left or right depending on the orientation of the atoms in the molecule. Hence the terms left-handed and right-handed.

What is interesting is that, when the amino acids in question are synthesised in the laboratory, the left- and right-handed structures always appear in a 50/50 ratio. Even more fascinating is that, should a right-handed type of amino acid end up in a living organism, it is immediately destroyed by enzymes. And things get even more peculiar when an organism dies: then the molecules generally rearrange themselves towards a 50/50 ratio.

The same left-right phenomenon occurs with nucleic acids, a different kind of molecule which is essential for the formation and maintenance of living organisms. Nucleic acids (the NA of DNA) are groups of so-called amine molecules. Of the infinitely many conceivable structures only four amines appear in living organisms and, in this case, all four are right-handed.

The exclusive choice of a very limited number of specific amino acids and amines and their exclusive optical one-handedness are two of the unsolved mysteries of biochemical evolution. They are examples of what

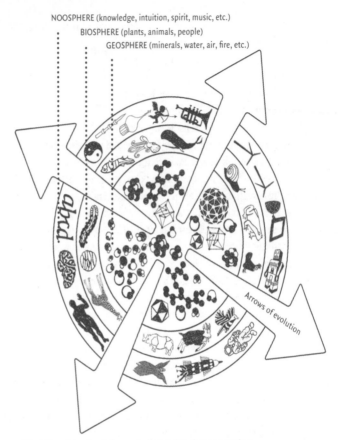

NOOSPHERE (knowledge, intuition, spirit, music, etc.)
BIOSPHERE (plants, animals, people)
GEOSPHERE (minerals, water, air, fire, etc.)

02) Evolution of planet earth from geosphere via biosphere to noosphere

I call minor mysteries, whose mechanism keeps repeating itself in the course of evolution unlike the unique mystery of the emergence of life.

An intriguing and unanswered question is how and when the above purely chemical building blocks led to life for the very first time. There was great excitement when, in 1952, experiments conducted by the American scientists Miller and Urey, the Russian Oparin and the British Indian Haldane showed that, under certain conditions relating to temperature, lightning and water, the kind of molecules present in the early phase of the earth could form amino acids, the building blocks of genetic material. It led to the conclusion that it must have been possible for life to emerge from such a 'primeval soup'.

Not at any time or place has anyone observed life emerge spontaneously.

This conclusion seems premature. If life at that time emerged from a primeval soup, then it could have happened more often, at different moments and different places, under similar conditions. But not at any time or place, including the past fifty years of intensive laboratory research, has anyone observed life emerge spontaneously under certain conditions. And not from such a primeval soup either.

A unique event

At the beginning of 2009, the Royal Society held an international conference in London for scientists who study the origin of life. They found that there are no convincing theories or successful experiments which give insight into how life could actually have emerged in such a primeval soup. It was confirmed that nobody has ever witnessed the spontaneous generation of life at any place or at any time.

The same observation was the great merit of the French microbiologist Louis Pasteur around 1850. He demonstrated with experiments in nature that everywhere, including in pure and clean mountain air, there are microbes, invisible to our eye, which for example cause milk to go sour and beer to ferment. At that time, the prevailing opinion was that this happened because of the spontaneous generation and subsequent propagation of living microbes in food. Pasteur's discovery also applies in a broader sense: life only comes from life.

So when did life begin? The first unicellular living organism? Nobody knows. We know all about the chemistry, physics and genetics of living organisms, but nothing about the origin of life. Biology has not even been able to determine what life really is.

As far as I can tell, in considerations on the emergence of life, there is hardly any mention that the event might have been a one-off occurrence. If it could be shown empirically that it is chemically possible under certain conditions for a molecule to emerge which reproduces itself and enables propagation, then the question arises: Why should it happen only once? Why not in a variety of different places on earth? Or in the laboratory? But there is no such evidence. As yet the emergence of life is a unique event without anyone knowing why or how.

Proving that life has also emerged elsewhere in the universe is of course challenging and relevant to the question of uniqueness. To this end, the SETI (Search for Extraterrestrial Intelligence) Institute was set up in California in 1984 in collaboration with the University of California at Berkeley. Here, scientists have been looking for signs of life in the universe using increasingly refined telescopes, so far without any success. In 2008, they held a workshop called 'The Sound of Silence' on the question of 'Are we alone?'. The answer was: 'We don't know.' Because of a lack of funding, the radioscopic research at SETI was put on hold in April 2011.

Our estimate that life on earth must have originated 3.5 billion years ago has been supported by most biologists in the last few decades and is based on the earliest fossils with elements of life which have been found in the region of the Pilbara hills in Western Australia. But we have never been able to identify a moment, place or condition where life emerges or has ever emerged spontaneously. This is the crux.

The idea that life emerged gradually does not seem to be a sensible option. There is life or there is no life. We do not know any intermediate forms, except that viruses are sometimes referred to as such. Viruses however are inanimate organic crystals which contain basic DNA material but cannot reproduce without 'borrowing' life from other living organisms. So here, again, life comes from life and not purely from chemistry.

Life can be frozen by rapidly cooling down a living embryo or other small organism to liquid nitrogen temperature (-70° Celsius). At this temperature, the structure and organisation of the cells are kept intact in a state with practically no molecular motion and a very slow metabolism. The physico-chemical structure of living matter seems to hold the key to the long-term memory of living organisms.

This phenomenon was also observed in 1997 by James Clegg in brine shrimp eggs which had been dried at room temperature and could be revived after four years. But here *revival* is the key word: there was life and it returned on the basis of memory in the structure. There is no new life, but life from life.

Every transition from non-life to life, in laboratories or in nature, viruses included, requires the 'use' of an existing living organism. This also turned out to apply to the sensational creation of a bacterium with a synthetic genome by scientists at the J. Craig Venter Institute in the United States, announced in May 2010. The researchers were also involved in the Human Genome project. Upon careful reading of the research paper, it appeared that it was only possible to allow this bacterium to emerge by putting the genome into an

Life must have originated at some point in time and, so it seems, at just that one time.

existing – albeit synthetically simplified – living bacterium. Nevertheless, the Economist reported the news under the misleading headline AND MAN MADE LIFE.

Life must have originated at some point in time and, so it seems, at just that one time. That is where we and every other living organism all come from. But we are in the dark about that single moment of emergence and about why and how. Here, just as with the birth of the universe, there is a saltatory, one-off discontinuity rather than a missing link in a gradual process. There is a major mystery, a new phase in the evolution in creation.

The next steps

After this saltatory change, a long and slow process of gradual evolution again emerged, as was also the case after the emergence of the universe. Following the first living and non-nucleated cells (prokaryotes) with one chromosome pair, which still exist today as amoebae and bacteria, approximately 1.5 billion years went by before nucleated cells (eukaryotes) appeared – a big and sudden step forward in the perfection of the cellular model. It then took a further 1.5 billion years before another major and sudden leap to multicellular organisms occurred.

In the meantime, the non-nucleated unicellular organisms had reached their limit of stability in a maximum size of 0.001 cm and stopped evolving. It is interesting that these unicellular organisms are still the largest and most robust population on earth: they are everywhere and always present, including our body, where they constitute 90 per cent of all cells.

After the emergence of multicellular organisms, an explosive expansion of these organisms began around 500 million years ago, an expansion known as the Cambrian Explosion. Until that time, unicells, with one chromosome pair, multiplied through cell division, as is still the case today. In multicellular eukaryotic organisms, with several chromosome pairs, a new replication mechanism suddenly (?) became active after 1.5

billion years. Halved haploid cells – containing half of the chromosome pairs – united with the haploid cells of other cells to generate entirely new combinations, new individuals: the sex mechanism. No longer 'more of the same'.

A slow, linear process of reproduction was transformed into a non-linear exponential process of reproduction; hence the explosion. Then within a very short period, the basis was laid for the structures and properties of all other organisms which now live on earth: plants, trees, fish, reptiles, mammals – the formation of species. Approximately 250 million years later, there was a mass extinction of unknown cause, followed by the advent of the dinosaurs. This period ended seventy million years ago as a result of the impact of a mega meteor which caused another mass extinction, to be followed by evolutionary revival.

Evidently, the biological history of evolution on earth, already 3.5 billion years old, proceeded excruciatingly slowly and gradually in the first 3 billion years with enormous growth in size to be sure but with little innovation. The truly explosive evolution of species took place in 'only' a few relatively short periods in the last 500 million years. Given the relatively short time span, purely gradual evolution seems unlikely. It is more likely that gradual development alternated with major leaps of diversification.

Darwin

This is a good moment to examine Darwin's theory a bit further because it is so often associated with the concept of gradual evolution and the emergence of life and because there are so many misconceptions about the theory.

It is sometimes suggested that, with Darwin's theory of evolution, we have discovered the secret of life. But this is not the case. Darwin describes processes and mechanisms in the biological evolution on earth but not their origin nor the question of why. In his works, he explicitly distances himself from any such suggestion. He even writes that the emergence of life is a complete mystery to him. This is why I think his book is carefully called On the Origin of Species and not, as is sometimes incorrectly cited, The Origin of Species. Moreover, species is hardly the same as life.

Darwin assumed a slow, gradual, step-by-step evolution, a gradational development resulting from random mutations which were then screened through natural selection. On all three fronts, namely gradual, random and selective, his theory now seems to fall short as the sole explanation of biological evolution on earth. These shortcomings are present even in the subsequent Neo-Darwinian theory, which incorporates the mechanism of gene mutation not yet known in Darwin's day.

The notion that there is saltatory evolution alongside gradual evolution is a hypothesis which we have only recently been willing to discuss.

Gradual evolution

With his gradual evolution, Darwin builds on the work of Carolus Linnaeus, the Swedish botanist who in the 18th century mapped the plant kingdom in his *systema naturae* and who concluded from his research that *natura non facit saltus*, or nature does not proceed by leaps. But since the 1980s, palaeontologists no longer subscribe to a purely step-by-step theory because too many essential links are missing. We now know that these missing links cannot be explained by conjecturing that they have got lost in those long periods and that finding sufficient intermediate links in a gradual process is just a matter of time, a belief generally held until the 1980s. In the last few decades, intensive research into fossils has now produced so much data indicating the opposite that the theory of only a gradual process has become untenable. At least, this is the case for the macro evolution of new species.

At the micro level of evolution – adaptation and selection through variation of existing species such as observed by Darwin on the Galapagos Islands – the theory appears to be correct. But an extrapolation of the micro mechanism to the macro mechanism of evolution in order to explain the emergence of species, which Darwin speculated on but also considered a risky assumption, seems unwarranted. Darwin writes that, if saltatory evolution could be demonstrated in the future, his theory would collapse.

It is likely that he was partially right with the natural selection mechanism he postulated but that it only applies to periods of minor and final gradual change. The notion that there is saltatory evolution alongside gradual evolution is a hypothesis which we have only recently been willing to discuss. Modern palaeontologists believe that fossil research – which has made further progress in the last few decades – confirms the hypothesis.

The two diametrically opposed points of view of gradual evolution and saltatory evolution are epitomised by scientists like Richard Dawkins and Michael Behe. Dawkins represents the belief that complex organisms emerge according to the rules of *epigenesis*, by which an organism develops through progressive differentiation of an initially undifferentiated whole.

Epigenetics is about accelerated evolution as a result of the *regulation* of genes rather than the *mutation* of genes. Order, organisation and structure 'emerge' as by-products of rules which are obeyed individually and locally, rather than rules followed generically. Dawkins calls this a kind of programming, a self-assembly by individual cells based on purely local rules. If this is the case, then we are no longer talking about gradual spontaneous evolution but about deterministically directed evolution. Dawkins does not explain where those rules and that determinism come or derive from. In *The Greatest Show on Earth*, he indeed says that we cannot answer the question of where we can find the source of the initial instructions (information) needed to design living complexity. It seems to me that this is in fact the acceptance of a mystery, even if 'deterministic' may sound more mechanistic than mysterious.

Behe presents his views in *The Edge of Evolution: The Search for the Limits of Darwinism*. He gives concrete examples of complex biological systems in nature, which in his opinion science cannot explain satisfactorily. He then argues that this is evidence of intelligent design. As a religious man, he relates this observation to the existence of God. In doing so, I feel that he goes to the opposite extreme and has provoked criticism from many other, including religious, scientists. But it seems out of the question that evolution is purely gradual.

Chance

The second element of Darwin's evolution theory is randomness or chance. Of the infinitely many combinations offered by atoms and molecules to form organic compounds and groups, about 1500 are instrumental to life on earth. These combinations, in turn, use only about 50 simple, organic molecules, including primarily the amino acids, amines, nucleic acids and proteins mentioned earlier. It is not possible to explain how this selection was drawn purely by chance from the billions of alternative initial combinations. Moreover, this experiment cannot be repeated and so the hypothesis is not scientific by definition.

Let me give an example to illustrate why chance alone is not a realistic option. The simplest protein molecule in living organisms is insulin, consisting of 51 combinations of amino acids constructed in a particular sequence. Since there are 20 basic amino acids, a probability calculation shows there is a 1 in 10^{66} chance of forming the given combination in the given order. This implies that on average a mixture of 20 amino acids requires one million trillion trillion trillion trillion trillion trillion attempts before it will achieve the configuration of insulin.

If we rely on chance alone, then the probability that a 'simple' bacterium will form is roughly 1 in 10^{40}.

And then we are just talking about the simplest protein. You do not need a strong imagination to realise that the configurations which will lead to the emergence of all the proteins needed to form and maintain complex living organisms cannot possibly be the result of chance alone.

Another example is what is known as *irreducible complexity*, a principle that continues to be fiercely debated to this day. The principle states that certain complex structures in nature cannot be reduced to a collection of individual parts which originated step by step through chance. Random mutations in living cells are the result of flaws in the fabric of the hugely complex process of transfer and reproduction and can sometimes speed up the evolutionary process but, in practice, mutated genes generally seem to be malignant and/or disappear. Furthermore, we have discovered that processes are triggered in and by the cells of the organism in order to destroy the abnormalities.

I will not go into all the detail of the battle raging amongst scientists, including Dawkins and Behe, over this subject. The principal question is whether there was enough time and whether sufficient building blocks evolved independently to create the first amazingly complex and coherent organs and organisms through an unobservable process involving the assembly of those building blocks. If we rely on chance alone, then the probability associated with the formation of the first minuscule 'simple' bacterium (which nonetheless contains 10^{10} atoms) amounts to roughly 1 in 10^{40}. So other mechanisms and factors must play a role. There continue to be heated discussions and publications on the subject even though nobody can prove they are right because the initial conditions of evolution cannot be reconstructed.

Human individuals after conception grow very rapidly from a fertilised cell into a super-complex organism, a process which can be explained from a given genetic database. The riddle of irreducible complexity, however, is about the initial emergence of the organ or organism in the evolution of

It appears that the eye emerged at least 40 times in the evolutionary process, independently and in many different forms.

species and not the evolution of species once the initial conditions are known.

A well-known subject in this context is the eye, an incredibly complex and coherent organ. Figure 03 gives a visual impression of the processes which take place between the eye and the brain to register observations. We now know – 150 years after Darwin's publication – that all organisms with eyes (from fly to human being) have a 'master gene' in their genome, called Pax6, which is responsible for directing cells in the formation of the eye. It also appears that the phenomenon of the eye emerged at least 40 times in the evolutionary process, independently, in different places and in many different forms. So it was not a gradual development from a single and simple start.

An impressive instance is the emergence 450 million years ago of the eye in the trilobites – one of the first organisms from the Cambrian Explosion – with a mind-boggling degree of perfection and with special underwater lenses. You would need to have rock-solid faith in Darwin's theory if you are to explain an organ which emerged in such a relatively short time through a gradual and accidental process.

It remains a mystery to me how certain very complex organs and organisms could have emerged from a sequence of purely mechanistic, chemical and physical processes, without direction from anywhere other than a material, genetic source.

Natural selection

The third pillar of Darwinism is the mechanism of natural selection. It seems to me that natural rejection would actually be a better expression because the mechanism does not select the best, i.e. the fittest, but rejects defective forms. The survivors then fit their environment best but they are not necessarily the strongest.

In discussing the gradual and chance aspects of Darwinian theory and their implausibility, I suggested above that other mechanisms probably play a role in this phase of biological evolution, such as evolutionary 'short cuts' originating from the inside of organisms rather than adaptations from the outside. I found corroboration for this hypothesis in a book published in 2010 by Jerry Fodor and Massimo Piattelli-Palmarini called *What Darwin Got Wrong*. It details new insights from developmental biology into evolutionary mechanisms. The authors' principal thesis is that endogenous – or internal – processes within living cells are primarily responsible for the emergence of species and forms whereas exogenous – or external – factors play a secondary role. The book thus relegates the 'natural selection' factor as well as the concepts of 'gradualism' and 'chance' to secondary roles.

Endogenous processes within living cells are primarily responsible for the emergence of species and forms.

The endogenous factors effect a pre-selection of possible forms and species. This could occur through epigenesis, mentioned earlier, or via 'horizontal' gene transfer ('jumping genes') between cell molecules, a phenomenon discovered very recently. Or robust 'master genes' may have steered the formation of organisms and organs for hundreds of millions of years.

In addition, physical, chemical and mathematical conditions have been discovered which impose internal constraints on the ultimate external forms emerging from cells. I will not go into the mechanisms in any detail but Fodor and Piattelli-Palmarini describe and substantiate them extensively.

The forms ultimately emerging from these internal evolutionary mechanisms then either fit or do not fit in with the natural environment in which the organism finds itself. That natural environment does not select but either does or does not provide accommodation, which is selected by the organism. Only then can any fine-tuning take place through a process of selection, as postulated by Darwin.

This new story of the evolutionary mechanism, known as the *evo-devo* mechanism (from evolution-development) in professional circles, seems to largely determine the emergence of species and forms.

The mystery of the inside
The history of evolution again seems to revolve around an endogenous inside and an exogenous outside and their interaction rather than only an outside which, in the days of Darwin, played a principal part in what were then new ideas on the mechanism of evolution. Knowing now that internal

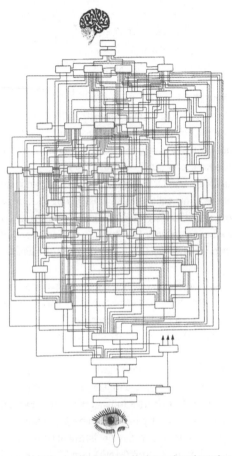

03) Processes which take place between eye and brain to register observations: an artist's impression

factors play a dominant role in the evolutionary mechanism, we are confronted with a picture that is new and surprising because we do not understand how the complex internal and interactive mechanisms of selection and restriction operate within the cells nor where they get their basic information.

At the end of their book, Fodor and Piattelli-Palmarini invite the reader to ask them what the mechanism of evolution is if the mechanism posited by Darwin is largely rejected. Their answer is: we do not know. They argue that nobody knows exactly how species emerge via infinitely many different routes and complex internal mechanisms, through continual surprises and not least through historically accumulated patterns.

The primary driver of natural selection is not the environment but internal gene regulation.

The authors expressly state that their book is not about God, Mother Earth, fairies or other 'pseudo-agents', but about the chemical, physical and mathematical basis of evolution. Why are they so desperate to avoid a confrontation with what at source is a mystery? Based on what intensive research has uncovered and published to date, it seems that the conventional views about gradualism, chance and natural selection do not come close to explaining the genetic, biological evolution of life on earth.

What are we made of?

This is an opportune moment for a few words on the subject of genetics. In 1952, James Watson and Francis Crick discovered the structure of a molecule in the nucleus of a cell, known as the Double Helix, a DNA molecule where all genes are embedded in chromosomes and which determines the characteristics and functioning of a living organism. For a brief moment, there was a glimmer of hope that we might yet find the answer to the question of what life is and where it comes from. As will become clear, it did not turn out that way.

Our body contains approximately 100,000 billion cells and every second we make 4 million new cells. Only 10 per cent of the total are the body's own cells. The remaining 90 per cent, as pointed out earlier, are bacterial cells. Every one of our own cells contains the entire human DNA molecule which, we now know, contains 26,000 genes and, stretched out, appears to be over one metre long. It is made up of strings of thousands of different sequences of the 64 possible triplet combinations of 4 specific amines, known as the base chemicals cytosine (C), guanine (G), adenine (A) and thymine (T).

To draw an analogy, the 4 amines are like the letters of the genetic alphabet, the 64 combinations are the words (there are 3 billion words in our body) and, in the genes, words are combined into sentences. The sentences contain the codes for the recipes which produce all the protein molecules (enzymes, hormones, etc.) in our body, made up of the 20 specific amino acids referred to earlier in this chapter. Somewhat disconcerting is the finding that, of the 26,000 genes, only about 2 per

Our body contains about 100,000 billion cells and every second we make 4 million new cells.

cent perform the essential active functions in the processes of life and that the bulk of the DNA molecule does not seem to have a clear function. The 98 per cent consisting of non-coding genes are also known as 'junk' genes. It has recently been discovered that they may well play a supportive role but this is by no means clear. Interestingly, the percentage of non-coding genes is often lower in organisms other than human beings! It is only 10 per cent for bacteria, for example, and 80 per cent for fruit flies.

The chemistry of the active genes produces chemical products for the supply of the complex chemical building blocks constituting our body. How that chemistry passes on the information is a puzzle. In recent decades, we have been able to improve our picture of how DNA functions but we have no idea how the double helix acquires the information it passes to the genes. Nor do we know how that information and the codes derived from it have led to the millions of different species found in nature and to the forms and shapes in which they appear, as well as other specific attributes such as colour and smell. We have figured out that the incredibly sophisticated process of information transfer proceeds from cell to organism but not how and where that information originated nor why and how that resulted in millions of species and forms.

A perfect example of the unbelievably complex functioning of our body concerns the role of water. We have discovered in more and more detail what the basic function of water is in cell biology, in genetic information transfer and in communication within our nervous system. I find this so interesting that I would like to say something about it.

The water molecules in our body constitute a coherent whole in liquid crystal form. This discovery has given us a completely new picture of the holistic communication network within our body. The most common protein in our body (70 per cent) is called collagen, a tripeptide made of amino acids proline, hydroxyproline and glycine. Collagen is a key basic building block (35 per cent) of our bodily tissue. All the water in our body (70 per cent of our mass) together with collagen constitute an orderly network via chemical and physical links, a liquid crystalline continuum. This continuum is the medium which, like a kind of hologram, reflects all the information circulating in the body via genes and neurons. It is through this medium that lightning fast messages are transmitted almost instantaneously, usually without our knowledge. I have experienced that, if you lie in bed very quietly and imagine yourself separate from the individual parts of your body, it seems to feel like a liquid crystalline whole.

Water is more than a molecule; it is an essential and participatory building block of living organisms.

In this network of collagen, water molecules are present in three forms, namely free, bound and an intermediate form trapped within the tissues. And each of these forms has its own structure and its own purpose. The entire network forms a coherent intracellular electric continuum for communication throughout the whole body. In other words, water is more than just a molecule, more than a commodity. It is an essential and participatory building block of living organisms.

Ingenious energy conversion

Another example of the ingenious design of our organism is that energy conversion occurs with an efficiency of almost 100 per cent because there is almost direct interaction between energy-consuming and energy-producing activities. These activities all proceed via the energy-absorbing ADP (adenosine diphosphate) molecules and the energy-supplying ATP (adenosine triphosphate) molecules, which play an active role in the body's metabolic process.

In our technological world of human ingenuity, the conversion of energy – e.g. from heat to work or from heat to electricity – occurs with an efficiency of at most 70 per cent. We cannot do any better because heat conversion is never sufficiently integrated into a coherent and closed model to prevent the loss of heat.

The above examples give an idea of the magnitude and complexity of our own beautiful body, an absolute marvel working around the clock at full speed. It is something we hardly ever think about and so we are quite careless and generally nonchalant about the most complex and self-conscious organism known to creation.

Genes

When techniques were developed in 1990 to map the entire human DNA complex, the Human Genome project took off in 1991. There were high hopes that we would soon be able to penetrate the secrets of life and the functioning of the genes. The project was completed ten years later and the results were published by 2003. I suspect that only the insider crowd of scientists have read the material closely and, as far as I can tell, the general public have barely noticed.

The British general practitioner and renowned medical journalist, James Le Fanu, first made me see in his 2009 book *Why Us?* how completely unexpected the results from the project were and how it has led to completely new insights, upsetting existing conventional theories about evolution and genetics. The study also made clear that the question of 'What is life?' had again been left unanswered.

I will mention a number of salient points from the above research. It turned out that the human genome consists of 'only' about 26,000 genes. This was a surprise. Given the composition, complexity, size and characteristics of the human organism, something closer to 100,000 had been expected.

In the meantime, further research on the genome of other organisms has shown, for instance, that the number of genes is about 40,000 in the world of plants, about 13,000 for a fruit fly, 17,000 for a one-millimetre worm and between 500 and 8000 for a single-celled bacterium. This is all much more than expected. For mice and chimpanzees, the number of genes is practically the same as for human beings. These numbers indicate that genes cannot be the sole reason behind the enormous differences in complexity, form and attributes across species.

It also appeared that identical genes are multi-purpose: they have many different functions and are interchangeable in many different cells within the organism. And it seems that active genes serve mainly to supply enzymes, the basic building blocks for the organism and internal processes, but how genes determine the appearance or the nature of the organism is still unknown. No mechanism was discovered which could explain attributes and behaviour. The DNA molecule for all its complexity is still no more than a physics and chemistry manual for the delivery of chemical products and processes. The Human Genome project did not report anything on how these chemical products and processes determine the form and behaviour of an organism or where the necessary information comes from.

Nor did the project offer support for the theory of mutation resulting from transmission errors which are supposed to have led to gradual change and adaptation of a species. This phenomenon cannot be inferred from the composition of the genes encountered. The 98 per cent equivalence of the number of genes and general similarity between the genomes of humans, chimpanzees and even mice, notwithstanding the essential differences in their anatomy and in the size and faculties of their brain, justifies the conclusion that genes do not play a decisive role in such differences. This was also stated by Svante Pääbo, the leader of the Chimpanzee Genome project, when the results were published in 2005.

For mice and chimpanzees, the number of genes is practically the same as for human beings.

So we are left with the question of where the instructions and codes come from which led to a diversity of millions of species with completely different forms and habits, yet all originating from the same basic genes. It seems that random mutations cannot have played much of a role. Adaptation through natural selection certainly did, but this does not go very far in explaining the enormous diversity which nature displays on earth. But the information originally embedded in genes must have come from 'somewhere'.

Back to the inside

So far science has basically focused on studying the outside of life, bogged down in biochemical and physical processes. Partly through the stimulus provided by the Genome project, there is undoubtedly much more material still to be collected and knowledge to be acquired, teaching us many things about pathogenic mutations and their treatment. The latest developments in the area of stem cells, which we can take from a patient's skin and convert into an original, embryonic cell of our own without any malignant genes, are amazing and perhaps even a bit frightening.

However, the Human Genome project has shown that scientific research into the outside of things will not enable us to pierce the boundary with the genesis of life. This is also the conclusion stated in the Fodor and Piattelli-Palmarini book: The origin is to be found on the inside. But they, too, do not get beyond methods which are biochemical, physical and

You cannot find and enter the meta world with a rational and technical methodology.

mathematical. On the other side of that boundary lies a different world, I think. There lies the meta world, a place you cannot find and enter with a rational and technical methodology.

Although there is still a great deal of pioneering, scientific research on genomes being published – with important favourable implications for public health – there is not much hope that it will open up new perspectives about the exact nature of the link between genes, information and chemistry.

My conclusion from everything we have learnt is that in addition to mutation, chance, natural selection and, most of all, the newly discovered endogenous processes in the biological evolution of living nature, there is a pattern, a source of information from the meta world. If the first 10 billion years of chemical and physical evolution are so irrefutably based on a coherent pattern, then why should that have disappeared all of a sudden thereafter?

It should be clear by now that the emergence of life is a major and mysterious discontinuity in the evolutionary process.

Evolution marches on

In the course of biological evolution, the level of consciousness within organisms grew in line with the complexity of the organism. This gradual development went hand in hand with many new and more tightly knit forms of family ties, communities and organised structures. However, unlike the new models in earlier phases of evolution, they increasingly allowed participants to retain their identity. The hydrogen atom in the water molecule, for instance, no longer has an independent identity, but an ant in an ant hill does – albeit perhaps limited – and presumably a person in a family, community or organisation even more so.

So new models emerge of combinations of organisms where individual identity is retained. In this gradually proceeding process, with the degree of consciousness growing, the next discontinuity after the emergence of life appears, namely the phenomenon of a self-reflective consciousness.

This evolutionary phase is again more complex and less predictable than the previous phase. It continues to build on a preceding pattern, but with far more room for diversification, local and individual creativity, and conscious involvement by the participants in the evolutionary process.

7
The mind
A mysterious medium

The concepts of consciousness and self-reflective consciousness continue to be the subject of many philosophical discussions but there is no scientific agreement yet. Consciousness appears to be a phenomenon which is difficult to fathom and define and cannot be pinned down to any distinct moment of emergence. It relates to the interaction between the material and immaterial qualities of phenomena in creation. According to the so-called neuro calvinists, there is no consciousness, and our thoughts and actions are determined exclusively by the material neuronal configurations in our brain, based on the system of genes we receive at birth. Other neurologists have more subtle points of view and recognise an invisible and non-measurable medium outside of the brain which steers the processes inside the brain.

The broadest interpretation of consciousness, I think, is that assigned by Teilhard de Chardin in his law of complexity/consciousness. In his view, there exists a direct connection between the complexity of a material phenomenon in evolution and the degree of consciousness which unfolds at the same time. The law implies that, apart from animals and humans, even the most elementary particle, even a stone or a tree, has a minimal degree of consciousness invisible to the eye. Teilhard opines that immaterial and material manifestations come from the same 'primeval stuff'. In living organisms, he sees a gradual increase in the degree of consciousness as the organism grows in complexity, clearly observable in a qualitative sense. Complexity here means the entire quantity, quality and intricacy of the building blocks and internal configuration of a material phenomenon.

In human beings – the most complex living organism we know – the degree of consciousness appears to be the highest according to the above definition. Not only do human beings have many genes, but they have the largest brain (in proportion to body mass), the most extensive brain faculties and the most complex nervous system of all living beings.

The use of skull size and brain volume to determine brain capacity in the classification of mammals is not uncontroversial. It is more accurate to relate brain capacity to brain volume as a proportion of the size of its owner, giving what is known as the *encephalisation quotient* (EQ). But there is no question that the human brain displays a large number of new properties compared with earlier species, and that the emergence of these properties was irrefutably a one-off occurrence in the evolution of nature.

And together with this one-off jump in the development of the human brain, there was a one-off jump in human consciousness. This was the emergence of self-reflective consciousness, a level that differs from the simpler consciousness in plants and animals in the sense that the human individual has the ability, among other things, to think in abstract terms, think ahead, think back, think about himself, think about consciousness, think about evolution, speak a language and write in it, and create art using instruments. This self-reflective consciousness could also be called the mind. I think that, in the history of a slow and gradual process of evolution of consciousness in all phenomena in nature, the emergence of self-reflective consciousness in humans was a discontinuity similar to the emergence of the universe and of life.

The explosive growth of the human brain began around three million years ago if we take as a reference point our ancestor Lucy, an intact skeleton of an *Australopithecus afarensis* female, dating back to that time. Since then the volume of the brain has grown from about 400 cubic centimetres to about 1600 cubic centimetres for *Homo sapiens*, or human beings today. Such growth is incompatible with Darwin's theory of evolution, which assumes that evolution on earth proceeds slowly and gradually, results from random mutation and is steered by natural selection. Relatively speaking, the growth of the brain proceeded so rapidly that it can certainly not be explained through a slow and gradual process. To the contrary, there was a relatively short lived period of saltatory growth.

The Human Genome project has shown that no permanent random mutations of any significance could have occurred via genes in such a short period. This conclusion is also apparent from the fact that the genome of a chimpanzee hardly differs from that of a human even though the volume and functions of the brain differ fundamentally. There is no convincing proof in the human history of that period – just a jumble of disconnected facts with a minimum of evidence – indicating that the growing size of the brain and a more developed intelligence played any clear role in natural selection. We can only speculate.

And it was hardly an advantage that the brain grew so rapidly that physical adaptations were needed, such as the mother's larger pelvis and a longer period of brain growth continuing until after birth. The development of the brain in a human baby cannot be completed until 18 months after birth because the pelvis, despite its growth, is still too small to accommodate the skull with a fully developed brain. At birth, the size of the brain is 23 per cent of its ultimate size. With chimpanzees, the pelvis has not grown but is large enough to allow the fully grown but smaller brain to pass through at birth.

The literature on the evolutionary history of our brain does not give us much concrete information because fossil findings during those few million years are very sporadic. What is clear however is that the growth in brain volume by 50 per cent in the last million years must have occurred very quickly.

Self-reflective consciousness
With the emergence of self-reflective consciousness, a gradual process in the biosphere suddenly ushered in an entirely new evolutionary phase: a jump to the noosphere. The noosphere is a concept developed by Teilhard de Chardin and referred to earlier. It is the medium where human knowledge and skills are stored via the brain and mind and are transferred directly between people without the delays inherent in a chronological progression of generations and genes.

The speed of the evolutionary process via the immaterial sphere is breathtaking. By way of comparison, whereas people's power of vision has not changed in many thousands of years, and has perhaps even deteriorated somewhat, we have in the last one hundred years improved our vision greatly by designing microscopes and telescopes which can penetrate deeply into the micro and macro worlds.

The emergence of self-reflective consciousness in humans constitutes a new, major discontinuity.

As I see it, the emergence of self-reflective consciousness – of the mind – in the human race constitutes a new, major discontinuity in the course of evolution. In particular, the unique and essential gift of language and writing embedded in our brain cannot be put down to a gradual evolutionary process. The genes which direct and transfer these characteristics have now been identified, but the sudden appearance of a very specific variant of the FOXP2 gene, approximately 200,000 years ago and only in *Homo sapiens*, cannot be reduced to a gradual process.

Attempts to teach animals with a relatively high degree of consciousness (e.g. dolphins, whales, chimpanzees, bonobos and orang-utans) human abilities such as the use of language and self-recognition have to my knowledge failed so far. The communication and recognition tools used by animals among themselves do not go beyond sounds and gestures, no matter how refined, differentiated and meaningful they may be.

It is unlikely that noises and gestures which clearly communicate something, such as the purring of a cat, barking of a dog, or singing of a bird, are the predecessors of language, reading and writing. The processes in the brain of *Homo sapiens* associated with these abilities are so complex and unique that they cannot have emerged from a gradual process: there almost certainly must have been a discontinuity.

The fact that Neanderthals, who had not quite disappeared when *Homo sapiens* arrived, had a higher EQ but do not seem to have had the gift of language, again points away from a gradual process. Also, it appears that the genetic composition of Neanderthals essentially differs from that of *Homo sapiens*, who was therefore not an immediate successor.

In any event, a sudden transformation resulted in the emergence of self-reflective consciousness and the associated special mental capacities in humans and we do not know how and where, only approximately when, it happened. Self-reflective consciousness is a mystery of an immaterial phenomenon emerging from a material setting.

Early as well as modern philosophers have occupied themselves with the question of whether and how this immaterial phenomenon could have emerged from matter. Dualists, such as Descartes and his followers down to the present day, maintain that immaterial phenomena do not exist and everything is matter. Monists, such as Spinoza and his disciples, assume that everything originally came from primordial matter and, as a result, mind and matter are inextricably connected. The latter hypothesis is also known as panpsychism. In this view, all matter has a mind-like quality and the mind cannot have emerged from matter all of a sudden.

In 2006, the British philosopher Galen Strawson constructed an interesting argument in *Consciousness and its Place in Nature*, which includes extensive comments from contemporaries and his response. He postulates

04) Growth of the brain

that all our concrete experiences – both material and immaterial – are realistic, physical phenomena, not to be confused with phenomena from physics. Given this view, physical phenomena also have an immaterial basis emanating from the above primordial matter.

The neurosciences have seen enormous progress, in particular through new scanning techniques which make it possible to look inside the brain of living beings and so follow the dynamic processes taking place there in communication with the body and the outside world. We have been able to map the entire human brain, measuring approximately 1600 cubic centimetres, and pinpoint the exact regions in the brain associated with sight, smell and hearing. We now know about the signals received by the brain and transmitted to the remotest corners of the body, leading to action, reaction and the storage of data (our memory).

The billions of neurons (nerve cells) in the brain and many more billions of links which operate neurological processes in the brain are equivalent to computer hardware totalling billions of modern PCs. So that is what human beings have available throughout a lifetime without realising it.

Who's the boss?
Now that we know this, the question is: What directs the system? Where does the software come from and how is information transferred? *Are* we a body or do we *have* a body? *Are* we our brain or do we *have* a brain?

Are brain and spirit, body and soul, matter and mind radically different worlds? We have not been able to agree for centuries. Descartes thought they were, while Spinoza thought they were not. And opinion remains divided to this very day.

Until recently, the connection between mind and brain was expected to be found in the physical structure of the brain. In this view, the human brain with its supercomputer capacity determines (through our genes) our perceptions, our reactions and our choices, in other words, our behaviour. Our mind is a derivative, managing our daily lives, our meso world. But overall control is left to the brain. This was, and to some degree still is, the prevailing opinion of neurologists.

How does it work?
We have studied the material processes of the brain with expert skill and have been able to chart the bulk of those processes. Just the map itself is

Are we a body or do we have a body? Are we our brain or do we have a brain?

a first-class miracle. Equally impressive is the literature describing how we now think that sensory impressions are collected and screened within the splendid isolation and darkness of the skull, reorganised and transmitted to the nervous system, which then provides us with a picture of how the brain interprets the outside world. Our perception of reality is determined in the grey mass of our brain. But what kind of reality is that?

Recent studies show that cerebral activity during the processing of an observation begins in the relevant region of the brain and then spreads to all other parts. When test subjects are confronted with one specific signal, a brain scan shows electrical flickering throughout the brain. In other words, information processing does not occur in isolated regions operating autonomously but involves the entire brain network.

Furthermore, it appears that the regions responsible for vision and hearing record observations by the eye and ear in approximately thirty different subregions, probably because the image is too complex to be processed within a single segment. The complete image then needs to be reassembled from these subregions so that a meaningful signal can be transmitted to the nerves. The location where the assembly takes place has not yet been identified and remains an unsolved puzzle. So contrary to what was thought until very recently and is often thought even today, the brain is a complex and coherent whole which cannot simply be reduced to regions.

The big mystery is how the billions of atoms, molecules and electrons making up the electrical circuitry and chemical processes continuously convert the information in our brain to and from the infinitely many immaterial, personal, and sometimes irrational, perceptions, ideas and feelings, such as affection, musical enjoyment, passion, compassion, doubt, inspiration, art as well as scientific and social innovation; that is, all the subjective and personal emotional experiences in our human existence, most of which cannot be measured or charted.

We fail to see anything special in all those ordinary atoms, molecules and electrons which seem to process the information via 'codes' in the organism. In Chapter 6, I stated that in the DNA molecule the four kinds of amine molecules can be seen as 'letters', the combination of amines as 'words' and the genes as 'sentences'. This metaphor is appealing but misleading because the language used to direct the organism is very different from the language spoken by people. Human language is based on agreements and familiar transfer mechanisms. Genetic language does not involve any agreement or familiar means of transfer. And it is puzzling how the chemistry and physics of ordinary molecules linked together in strings and in a certain sequence make the unspoken 'DNA language' work.

Our perception of reality is determined in the grey mass of our brain. But what kind of reality is that?

We do not have an explanation of how measurable, material processes in the brain are translated to and from non-measurable, immaterial processes in the soul, consciousness, heart, mind or whatever you choose to call it. We feel in ourselves a connectedness between our emotions and body, between our thoughts and actions and between the immaterial and material. But we do not know how it works.

We also sense that somewhere resides our autonomous, own self, our unique personality, our own character and our experience of things we see, smell, feel and hear – not some vague notion but the everyday reality of the meso world. Every single one of the seven billion people currently on our planet and their predecessors is and was a unique personality with an individual mind and personal 'software' determining an individual exterior appearance and an individual character, with room for innovation. What is the role of neurons in these experiences and how do they fulfil that role?

Just keep looking
After everything we had and had not discovered about the workings of the human brain – to date the most complex phenomenon in the universe familiar to us – the time was ripe in 1990 for a step to a larger, concerted and globally coordinated, comprehensive study: the Decade of the Brain. The official proclamation on the Decade of the Brain project of the Library of Congress, signed by then-US President George Bush Sr, opened with the following sentence: 'The human brain, a 3-pound mass of interwoven nerve cells that controls our activity, is one of the most magnificent – and mysterious – wonders of creation. The seat of human intelligence, interpreter of senses, and controller of movement, this incredible organ continues to intrigue scientist and layman alike.'

We feel a connectedness between our emotions and body but we do not know how it works.

This applies not only to 'the' brain of 'the' human individual but also to the specific brain of every single person. The primary project plan was to contribute to the identification of and to advance cures for brain abnormalities and damage, both congenital and accidental. A secondary objective was to discover how material processes are translated to immaterial sensations and vice versa.

Despite an enormous refinement of our map of the physical structure of and processes within the brain, there has been a growing gap between the concepts of matter and mind since 1990. We now know much more about the configuration of the brain and much less about the configuration of the mind. The link between the two continues to be a puzzle, a mystery. With the Decade of the Brain, we are even further from resolving the issue than we were a century ago. This was stated by John Maddox, former chief editor of *Nature*, a leading scientific journal, in a lecture given after the completion of the research in 2001.

I remember that, when Rupert Sheldrake published his 1981 book *A New Science of Life: The Hypothesis of Formative Causation*, *Nature* branded it as 'a book to be burnt'. I think *Nature* was too conservative at that time to share Sheldrake's vision of a connectedness between matter and non-matter in invisible fields in the universe or, what he calls, morphogenetic fields. Now, some 30 years later, we are heading in that direction and *Nature* no longer resists the growing signs that modern physics is starting to venture close to the boundary with metaphysics. The link between the physics, chemistry and electronics of the brain and the metaphysics of the mind also touches such a boundary.

We can ascertain ourselves that there is such a connectedness because we experience the interactions personally. This is not a theory but daily practice and explains why Strawson in *Consciousness and Its Place in Nature* calls concrete immaterial experiences a physical reality.

To have or to be
An intriguing question is whether the immaterial software of our immaterial mind exists independently of our material brain – the viewpoint of the dualists. An interesting fact here is that most cells in the body, so almost our entire body, are largely replaced about once a year (heart and brain cells are

replaced much more slowly). Ultimately, this process of replacement comes to an end through old age and wear and tear, but information and energy keep coming in which is important to keep down the level of entropy and maintain the organism.

As I tried to explain earlier, the information required to generate new cells for the body comes from our genes and not from our brain. If there is no information from our genes, there is no cell replacement. The body is completely dependent on information which flows from our genes to our brain, and not the other way round, and which originates from an unidentified source.

When we injure ourselves, our brain relays signals telling us to take actions that will heal the injury. At the same time, our genes immediately, but without our knowledge, start making the right cells to repair the local injury and stop the loss of blood. For certain living creatures, such as salamanders, a body part lost through injury can be fully regenerated because the software is available in its entirety. In principle, this is also possible for human beings although it does not usually work in that way because the instructions from the brain to stop the bleeding and close the wound lead to actions by ourselves and by 'regenerating' genes. This is faster than replacing the entire body part and stops any reconstruction.

So we *are* not our body at all, as the body disappears and is more or less replaced on a regular basis. We *have* a temporary body, albeit one that keeps growing older. Our software, our individual identity or our creativity, is available 'somewhere' to produce cells via our genes. And that source is used for that purpose as long as we live. One day we will die and a lifeless material carcass will remain, which will quickly decay and disintegrate as the atoms and molecules look for new accommodation.

It is often said that, upon death, the soul leaves the body but I think it is the other way round: when the body perishes, the body leaves the soul. And what happens then with our software, our consciousness, our mind? The notion that the brain is the exclusive driver of the mind seems to me an untenable assumption. The opposite is much more likely. In neither case, however, does there appear to be any prospect of a scientific explanation for the way in which the process of content transfer between mind and matter works. And where do the initial information and creativity – the software which determines our essence – come from? From the meta world? And does it return to that world when we die?

> It is often said that, upon death, the soul leaves the body but I think it is the other way round.

It is ultimately not possible to trace the source of the information responsible for steering all the biological processes. The same applies to the information and creativity received or transmitted by our mind and the brain. The emergence and existence of the mind, of self-reflective consciousness, including its relationship with the brain, thus continues to be a major mystery. Perhaps the EU Human Brain project announced in May 2011 will generate new insights. I think it will as far as diagnostics and surgery are concerned but I doubt whether we will unravel the mystery.

8
Restoring coherence

To recover our sense of coherence in the evolution within creation, it is important to understand how we began to lose it. Restoring it is essential if we are to meet the challenge of implementing a new model in 21st-century society.

Science has significantly enhanced our insight and information vis-à-vis the evolutionary process and its constituent parts. We have been able to map every evolutionary phase almost entirely from the moment there was a universe, from the moment there was life, and from the moment there was consciousness. Moreover, with the knowledge thus accumulated, we have been able to make enormous strides in the areas of technology and medicine. And as a result, we have been able to improve the quality of life for a great many people.

The previous chapters have shown that everything is interconnected in the process of evolution, which has lasted around 13.5 billion years and is still in full swing. While we as human beings have begun to understand the nature of the coherence better and better in the last few centuries, we are at the same time losing sight of that coherence due to an increasing degree of specialisation. I call this compartmental thinking.

At the same time, the extreme degree of specialisation in what are often complex disciplines has meant that we tend not to look beyond the boundaries of those disciplines. We may not see the opportunities and threats associated with any cross-disciplinary relationships. In the worst case, the threats we ignore may cause the collapse of entire structures, including economic, ecological and political systems as well as human individuals.

The danger of specialisation applies to the areas of medicine, social science, technology, business administration, finance and law – in fact, to all disciplines. Perhaps we have a vague idea that everything in life is generally connected but, in practice, interdisciplinary thinking and acting appears to be anything but simple.

Given the scale, speed, complexity, and impact of the growth in world population, compartmental thinking is a growing problem in our attempt to keep the global system intact. We are losing sight of any coherence while, oddly enough, we are becoming more interdependent.

The arts and sciences

An important stumbling block getting in the way of interdisciplinary thinking is the arts-science dichotomy of thought, especially in western society. Scientist and novelist C. P. Snow, in his now celebrated 1959 lecture in Cambridge, referred to this dichotomy as the 'two cultures', namely the 'sciences' and the 'humanities'. He points to this persistent division, deeply rooted in our educational system, as the strongest brake on a sustainable development of human – and particularly western – society. Some examples of the divide between the arts and sciences are intuition versus reason, spirit versus matter, belief versus knowledge, nature versus technology, ecology versus economy, and female versus male. And very often the divisions manifest themselves in diametrically opposed role models.

I became interested in the historical development of the duality between the sciences and humanities because it is closely tied in with the separate ways taken by science and nature and by science and religion. Better insight into the background to this division allows us to have another, different look at the interconnectedness in creation.

Antiquity and the Middle Ages

The origin of current philosophical thought can be traced back to a period between 800 and 200 BC, which gave birth to a completely new world view within a relatively short period of time, right across all of human society in the various continents, from East to West.

The philosophies of Socrates, Plato and Aristotle in Greece, the prophecies of Elijah, Isaiah and Jeremiah in Palestine, the dualism of Zoroaster in Persia, the revelations of Buddha and the Upanishads in India and the wisdom of Confucius and Lao Tzu in China are good examples. These ways of thinking shared a growing awareness of individual, critical reflection which to a certain degree was starting to replace the shamanic group mythology of the old tribes. It implied a shift of emphasis away from the group to the individual, including an individual perception of creation or the relationship with the Creator.

We are losing sight of any coherence, even though we are growing more interdependent.

Except for Taoism, this shift also led to a picture of two different worlds – one physical and the other metaphysical – with a varying degree of interconnectedness depending on the particular philosophy. The era witnessed a remarkably coincidental 'leap' in human thinking in various parts of the world and, in Karl Jaspers's 1949 book *Vom Ursprung und Ziel der Geschichte* (*The Origin and Goal of History*), is referred to as *die Achsenzeit* or the axial period. He meant an axis from Greece to China.

Plato and Aristotle saw a fundamental harmony in the universe, with Aristotle in particular regarding the universe as an organism. Both philosophers emphasised reason, idea, logos, or the immaterial as the ultimate and perfect reality. They believed that the material world consisted of imperfect phenomena. Aristotle to be sure showed more interest in the physical world and nature than his teacher Plato but nonetheless he believed strongly that reason and mind should prevail, continually emphasising the fundamental opposition between subject and object. This way of thinking had an enormous influence on subsequent, radically dualistic trends in scientific, philosophical and religious developments in the West.

Philosophical developments in the East, through Buddhism and Hinduism, were influenced by a similar, albeit less radical, distinction between the reality of the spiritual and the illusion of the material world.

The original philosophical view maintained by Taoism in China was different and unique because it did not lead to such a radical dualism. This is why Buddhism, though very influential, was never adopted in China in its original form. When Buddhism was introduced to China in the first part of the first millennium, it was adapted to the world-affirming harmonious model of Taoism. Readers familiar with the Chinese Taoist androgynous goddess Kuan Shi Yin will know that she 'originated' from the male bodhisattva Avalokiteshvara after 800 AD.

In the West, the Platonic and Aristotelian (and later Neoplatonic) ways of thinking led to an ambiguous combination of radical dualistic thought, on the one hand, and mystical experience, on the other, and were important elements in the later development of western science and Christianity. In the 13th century, Christian thought was set out by Thomas Aquinas in his *Summa Contra Gentiles*, written in the same period as *Summa Theologiae*. Both works are still the basis of Catholic doctrine today. They rest mainly on concepts and judgements, on logic and reason, on systematic and abstract thought, composed in the spirit of Greek philosophy and formulated in the spirit of legalistic Roman culture.

In the same period, Bonaventure, an influential Franciscan, professed a theological synthesis that was strongly influenced by Francis of Assisi's love of nature. Bonaventure believed in an inextricable connectedness between theology, mysticism and the everyday world, and accordingly played an important role in the rejection of a world view founded on radical dualism. His theological view is regarded as an embodiment of the principle of *coincidentia oppositorum*, or the coincidence of opposites which are linked because they are complements as well as substitutes, resembling what is symbolised by the Taoist principle of Yin and Yang. However, Bonaventure's thought was overshadowed by the enormous power and popularity of the views propounded by Thomas Aquinas.

After the Middle Ages, the western world gradually and increasingly shifted its attention to the material world. The reason for this shift lay in the separation between God and the world, and in the assumption that the world was directed from outside by means of a plan determined by God. To understand God's purposes and ways, western thinkers tried to get to know that plan by inventing and discovering 'laws' in the material world of nature. This was done primarily by analysing, subdividing and measuring that material, natural world and was the beginning of reductionism.

During this first period, the Church still followed science in terms of thinking in two separate worlds (physical and metaphysical) especially because scientists assumed that God was the Creator, in line with the doctrine of Thomas Aquinas, which assumed God to be the 'first mover'. But subsequent periods show an increasing divergence between Church and science.

The 16th and 17th centuries

The cultural divide between the sciences and humanities actually came about as early as the 16th century with the development of the scientific method of induction. According to this method, we design a theory or law and then test it against the real world. This contrasts with what is known as the deductive method, which first makes an observation in the real world and then derives a law (of nature). The first method revolves around mankind, the second around nature. Induction can be seen as an approach that fits in with the sciences and deduction as an approach that fits in with the humanities. The inductive, scientific approach was giving greater and greater insight into questions of 'how and why something is', and typified the cultural phase the West had arrived at. In the preceding phase, attention was primarily focused on 'that something is' and then 'what it is'.

In the development of scientific thought through the centuries, many discoveries were made. They often led to such a radical break with the traditional world view that scientists as well as philosophers were completely mesmerised. Examples of such discoveries include the emergence, age and position of the earth in the universe, the evolutionary development of life on earth, the reducibility of all macro and micro processes in creation to a single moment of emergence and, in the 20th century, the consistent patterns in the molecular structure of the cells in all living beings, the equivalence of energy and matter, and the relativity of time. All these discoveries led to seemingly unlimited technological developments and an improvement in human welfare and well-being.

In the 16th and 17th centuries, the increasing tension between the emerging natural sciences and the Roman Catholic Church is particularly striking. The hypotheses put forward by Galileo Galilei, inspired by the inductive method, gave new insights into the causality of motion. The empirical evidence that every object, regardless of weight, falls at the same rate seemed innocent enough. But the finding that the earth goes around the sun and is part of the solar system was in conflict with the world view conjured up by the Church that the earth and man are the centre of creation. The Church did not agree partly because it was narrow-minded and trying to protect itself and partly because it wanted to guard religious believers against confusion. As is well-known, the outcome was that in 1633 the Inquisition put Galilei on trial, demanding that he recant his theories. In 1992, so 359 years later, during a session of the Pontifical

The 17th century witnessed a shift in emphasis away from a divine plan towards material laws.

Academy of Sciences in Rome, Pope John Paul II officially declared that Galilei was right. In other words, a committee set up in 1979 had taken thirteen years to reach the conclusion that 'the Inquisition had acted in good faith but had drawn the wrong conclusions'.

There was one monastic order of the Roman Catholic Church which did not subscribe to the clash between the sciences and the humanities prevailing at that time. This was the Jesuit Order, an intellectual group who largely agreed with Galilei's argumentation and were able to place it in a dynamic model of creation theory. They were the same Jesuits set up as an order by the Roman Catholic Church to act as a kind of strike force (their leader has the title of 'general') against the reformation started by Luther. There does not, however, seem to be any other relationship between Luther's world of thought and that of Galilei. It is worth noting here that the Reformation movement (which was not so much directed at the authority of the Church as the improper use of that authority) had a far greater immediate impact on the people than the notions of Galilei, which affected only a small group.

The 17th century witnessed a growing shift in emphasis – greatly abhorred by the Church – away from a divine plan towards material laws. In the western world, a mechanistic view of the world (everything in the universe can be reduced to nothing but matter and motion) started to predominate. The early exponents of this movement, such as Isaac Newton and Francis Bacon, were deeply religious in their ways of life and thinking, and they were aware of the risks associated with their quest. But it was the age of exploration, both spiritually and geographically.

An increasingly pronounced shift towards a materialistic and mechanistic world view led to polarisation vis-à-vis the established traditions in religion and society. Exponents of the natural sciences developed a fascination which ended in a complete denial of any religious or mystical dimension (Laplace in the 18th century, Darwin in the 19th century and Monod in the 20th century).

The distance between the two ways of thinking was so great that there were hardly any efforts – not even any attempts at an effort – to bridge the gap. An additional problem nowadays is that a scientific way of thinking requires a high degree of specialisation and generally above-average intelligence so that most people can not relate to the world of science. This also explains why the gap which developed between religion and science continues to this very day in the conflict between the humanist-oriented religious creationists and science-oriented secular evolutionists.

The gap between religion and science continues in the conflict between religious creationists and secular evolutionists.

The 17th and 18th centuries

In the 17th and 18th centuries, mechanistic notions were further developed and refined by Newton, Descartes and Lagrange – still within a select circle – and led to the development of physics and chemistry. Mechanistic, materialist thinking predominated. It remains an open question whether this is the reason why we cannot find any exponent of humanistic thought in the 17th century, which seems to have a gap here.

The 18th century saw Jean-Jacques Rousseau protest against the prevailing balance of power in society. He postulated that art and science lowered people's standards of morality. Art and science were practised by a small intellectual elite who so much excelled in what they did that everyone else including those in power became idle and decadent. Rousseau therefore opposed both the arts and the sciences and wanted to go back to nature where there is no conflict between art and science.

His *Discours sur l'Origine et les Fondements de l'Inégalité Parmi les Hommes* (Discourse on the Origin and Basis of Inequality Among Men) and his ultimately famous central work *Du Contrat Social* (On the Social Contract) are both directed at unnatural and inappropriate tendencies in modern society. In these works, he not only opposes the arts and the sciences but also elitist and authoritarian positions of power. This resistance to power, knowledge and art continued into the next centuries, influencing the American War of Independence, the French Revolution and the Communist Manifesto.

The 19th century

In the 19th century, we see an interesting coincidence. On the humanistic side, Marx was developing his vision of a new social order, while on the scientific side Darwin was developing his theory on the origin of species.

> *In Darwin's theory, fittest does not mean strongest but best adapted to the environment.*

What they have in common is that both describe a dialectical process with elements of innovation. Marx recognised this common element: he regarded the scientific reasoning underlying the dialectical method in natural history as an underpinning of his thesis on dialectics in social history. He even invited Darwin to write an introduction to *Das Kapital* (*Capital*). Darwin did not want anything to do with it, expressly limiting himself to his own specific area of expertise and rejecting any personal relationship with or influence on social or religious domains.

The fact that a link was made – at least by Marx – was a first attempt to bridge the two cultures. A dialogue between Marx and Darwin, and thus a potential link between the arts and the sciences, foundered on Darwin's personal attitude, but might have been fascinating. Nor was Darwin willing to take a position on whether there was any direction in the system he had meticulously described and substantiated. He felt that the term evolution had certain associations and did not use it in his first writings. The same is true for 'survival of the fittest', a term which was incorrectly attributed to him and coined by Herbert Spencer, a contemporary English biologist and philosopher. In Darwin's theory, 'fittest' does not mean strongest but best adapted, i.e. 'fitting' the environment. This difference in interpretation has quite often led to misunderstanding, in Darwin's own day as well, such as the comparison of survival-of-the-fittest (but actually, survival-of-the-fitting) processes in nature to societal processes. The social Darwinists, with Spencer as a leading figure, were prominent exponents of such comparisons.

The 20th century

At the beginning of the 20th century, there was a major breakthrough in scientific thought with entirely new theories about the relationship between energy and mass, space and time, and gravity and the speed of light in the macro world, as well as electrical and magnetic forces, and particles and waves in the micro world. This led to a completely different view of the world and the universe. The mechanistic view of Newton was superseded. In addition, there were new waves of inventions and discoveries, especially in the areas of astrophysics, atomic energy, microelectronics, microbiology and quantum mechanics.

The two great geniuses who gave rise to these innovations were the pantheistically inclined Albert Einstein and the Taoistically inclined Niels Bohr. Although their theories were a breakthrough towards more interdisciplinary thought, the number of specialists and the number of disciplines continued to increase for the time being. Here we have a true paradox: while the realisation of a holistic coherence of everything in the universe was growing stronger, the 20th century developed into the 'century of specialisation' and so of increasingly compartmental thought.

On the one hand, progress in the sciences has allowed us to penetrate more deeply than ever into the structure of matter, organisms and the universe. We thus see that, in the past few decades, no fewer than 200 subatomic particles have been discovered, a far cry from the original concept of the atom ('atom' is derived from the Greek word for 'indivisible'). We now also know that the universe consists of at least 80 billion galaxies (such as the Milky Way) and that our sun with its own nine planets is just a tiny star in the midst of at least 30 billion trillion other stars. Moreover, we have discovered the chemical composition of the most complex components of life forms as well as the chemical and physical processes which maintain these organisms. We have been able to link a number of these processes to the functioning of our mind.

On the other hand, the nature of the methodologies giving rise to these discoveries – that is, the analytical separation of the objects of study into their various components – has led to a way of thinking which to some degree has caused us to lose sight of the interconnectedness between the earth, mankind, and the universe. In western society, the problem of isolation and limitation through specialist approaches is becoming very serious. The need to reestablish our sense of that interconnectedness is growing.

'Basing thought and action exclusively on science leads to technocratic solutions where people are treated as objects to be managed. Basing thought and action exclusively on values, without a thorough investigation of the real world and how it functions, leads to situations where what is realised differs from what those values aim to achieve.' This was a statement made in 1977 by A.G.M. van Melsen in *Geloof, Wetenschap en Maatschappelijke*

The need to recover our sense of interconnectedness is growing.

Omwentelingen (Religion, Science and Social Upheaval). It perfectly encapsulates the distinction between the arts and the sciences.

On the road to recovery

With this in mind, I would like to mention a few notions held by the palaeontologist and Jesuit Teilhard de Chardin, who in my opinion made an important contribution in the 20th century to the stimulation of interdisciplinary thought. He was far ahead of his time and the Church when, in the 1930s, he recorded his vision of evolution and creation in *The Phenomenon of Man*. The manuscript was published only after his death in 1955, much to the displeasure of the Vatican, which had tried to prevent its publication for twenty years.

Teilhard endorsed neither the humanities nor the sciences but, in his day, was one of the first advocates of a synthesis between the two modes of thought. Importantly, he established a link between the humanities and the sciences in the study of creation. He moreover pointed to the existence of an evolutionary, dynamic, cosmogenetic process with a direction and a growing degree of consciousness in more and more complex phenomena. A self-reflective consciousness in the phenomenon of man is the final culmination in biological evolution.

Teilhard's theological model emphasises a creative process of action rather than a passive process of salvation. It is a world-affirming rather than a world-rejecting view. Teilhard convincingly preached the active involvement of the individual in worldly occupations. Through his work on earth, man can achieve completion, become aware of the reality of nature, and contribute to the development of individual as well as collective consciousness. This then achieves two closely related goals: growth of the individual at a micro level and completion of the world at a macro level.

Teilhard noted that individual experience of growth and attachment in everyday life, on the one hand, and of withdrawal and detachment in spiritual life, on the other, are two aspects of the human world which we can reconcile. There is no irreconcilable contradiction which forces us to make a choice. These two elements of human existence – involvement in the practical (meso) world and devotion to the transcendental (meta) world – are inextricably connected.

In the West, after 2000 years of dialectical and often radically dualistic thinking about the earth, man and the universe, Teilhard's view – one that encourages convergence and harmony – is now helping to make us realise that unity and interconnectedness in evolution and creation must be restored. His view goes beyond compartmental thinking, and this is something we desperately need if we are to bring about the revolutionary social change required to prevent the human race from crushing the planet and seriously compromising the liveability of that planet in the 21st century.

Teilhard is helping us realise that interconnectedness in evolution and creation must be restored.

9
A discontinuity in the 21st century

The previous chapters have outlined evolution in creation since the birth of the universe, 13.5 billion years of impressive developments which have now taken us well beyond the threshold of the 21st century. The question arises as to where we currently stand in this evolutionary process. What phase have we entered, what is our role in that phase and what does it mean for our own and future generations? And most of all: what can we learn from the evolutionary developments of the past?

My journey of discovery has taught me that the 21st century will very likely witness a phenomenal tour de force. The ability of our planet to support human life is being pushed to the limit by the size of the population and concomitant consumption, pollution and depletion of irreplaceable raw materials. Two extreme scenarios present themselves. Either we go full speed ahead until we are struck by a catastrophe, ushering in an entirely new model; or we stay firmly in the driver's seat and completely redesign human society. Both scenarios represent a radical discontinuity.

I assume that the second scenario is preferable though the actual outcome might well be an intermediate one. Whatever the result, we will need all the ingenuity and innovative powers of our mind to face what will be an entirely new situation. It will require the realisation of a coherent global socio-economic order in the evolution of our planet. So what does that mean?

I will start at the beginning. In the first 10 billion years after the Big Bang, there was an inorganic evolution, giving rise to the earth at the end of the first 9 billion years. The emergence of life on earth 3.5 billion years ago initiated a period of organic, biological evolution. And the last 200,000 years have seen a cultural, spiritual evolution, after self-reflective consciousness emerged in human beings.

In this whole process, the speed of evolution has increased as the second phase is only a third as long as the first, and in this second phase, the biggest evolutionary push came in the final 500 million years. The third phase is now progressing at full speed and resulting in a range of phenomena, themselves growing at an exponential rate, which might lead to a breaking point in the course of the 21st century. If this trend continues, then – as can be seen from an extrapolation of the exponential trends depicted in Figure 06 on p. 104 – the discontinuity could lie somewhere between 2025 and 2040. How does this picture fit in with past patterns of evolutionary history and what does it mean for our future?

Breakthrough

We have seen that, in the course of the evolutionary process, there were certain key moments when a particular model reached its maximum manageable size. This was the case for the atomic model, the molecular model, the cellular model as well as the organismic model. When the largest but still coherent form was attained, a new and more complex model always emerged from the building blocks of the previous model.

This always meant drastic change in internal structure, active force fields, information transfer, form, the degree of consciousness and, increasingly, the model's interaction with its environment. Although the older building blocks – atoms, molecules and unicellular organisms – continue to exist on their own as part of the cosmic family, the more complex composite forms of organism and organisation have a decreasing lifespan. This is something we can now observe in the world of plants and animals, including human society. So unlike the older building blocks, these complex composite forms do not continue to exist independently. Not only do they die as individual specimens, eventually they also die out as a species.

This has implications for the future course of the evolutionary process because existing generations will not live to see new models and new generations will not personally encounter old models. Any evidence of the more complex models from the biosphere will be in fossil rather than living form. Only the human species will leave more and more fully documented evidence of past forms of life and will store and pass down ideas via the noosphere.

We have seen that, during the biological evolution of organismic species, the increase in their complexity was accompanied by a parallel increase in the degree of consciousness. And the gradual evolution of consciousness saw a parallel development (known as sociobiology) of cooperation, group formation and 'organisation' of various organisms in response to a growing social need. This progression from organism to organisation emerged in all living beings in the course of biological evolution insofar as there was a certain degree of consciousness in any given species. It resulted in many different kinds of group formation in the world of animals, humans included.

Human intervention

During that gradual process, a new discontinuity arose approximately 200,000 years ago, namely self-reflective consciousness, exclusively in human beings. It allowed them ultimately to invent and develop models themselves rather than simply being a consequence of a model. Humans have thus assumed the role of 'designer': they have become co-creative. Models now not only emerge, they are also designed. Here is a new motivator, a new engine of change and innovation in evolution. It is in this sense that the emergence of self-reflective consciousness in humans was a major discontinuity in evolution.

As far as we can make out at this moment, it seems that self-reflective *Homo sapiens* is the most complex, yet still coherent, manageable form of the physico-organismic model in the final phase of biological evolution. After a relatively short evolutionary process, the human organism in its physical form has not shown any refinement for a very long time. To the contrary, the human race might well be deteriorating given its growing susceptibility to illness and addiction. As yet we have been able to limit or alleviate these conditions through medical intervention as a result of our innovative mind. But the human organism as such may have finished evolving physically in terms of maximal feasible coherence. It has reached its physical limit.

The human species has not in the least finished evolving non-materially.

What is interesting however is that the human species has not in the least finished evolving non-materially. The discontinuity occurring approximately 200,000 years ago has led to inventions, discoveries, and innovations which in turn have greatly expanded the range of human senses, particularly in the past 50,000 years. In evolutionary terms, they have happened in an incredibly short time. In the last 100 years, this expansion has been exponential.

But these inventions and discoveries have also contributed to a likewise exponential population growth, a rapidly rising standard of living, and an avalanche of technological innovations. We have seen a corresponding acceleration in consumption, in the depletion of natural resources and in the pollution of the environment. At the same time, the potential capacity of computers to think and innovate is growing and may soon surpass that of the human brain.

This combination of simultaneous exponential developments seems to have moved beyond our control. On the one hand, we are growing exponentially towards a collective material maximum on earth as far as the resources of the planet are concerned. On the other hand, our global immaterial potential is also growing exponentially through an explosion of culture, knowledge and ingenuity. It appears that, after the recent discontinuity of self-reflective consciousness, another discontinuity is on its way. How that discontinuity will manifest itself we do not know, just as we did not know for previous discontinuities. But it is clear that we ourselves can play a decisive role in the process.

An amazing feat

In the meantime, we continue to develop our resourcefulness and innovative urge at great pace. The next 20 to 30 years will be a very exciting time – this is, after all, what the exponential trends are indicating. We will then see whether we will have the ingenuity to steer the nature of the discontinuity so that it will not simply 'emerge of its own accord'. We will have to counterbalance the exponential material evolution generated by ourselves with an exponential immaterial revolution, also generated by ourselves. It will be an amazing feat. The problem is that this discontinuity will probably occur not a few billion or a few million or a few hundred thousand years from now but more likely a few decades from now. This is extremely soon. Either the exponential developments will explode or they will level off in time, as is tentatively happening with the current growth in population. Both scenarios, however, involve a drastic change in the design of human society. We need to prevent matters from getting out of hand. How are we going to manage that?

Our track record

If we look back on how we have dealt with this challenge in the last four decades or so, there is not much reason for optimism as yet. During the second half of the 20th century, it began to dawn on us that the human world population was growing exponentially. By the turn of the century, expectations were confirmed: that in the previous one hundred years the world population had grown by about 5 billion people, from just over 1.5 billion in 1900 to more than 6.5 billion in 2000. And in November 2011, we reached 7 billion. Even today, there is an increase of more than 70 million people per annum. The growth rate is slowly decreasing so that, later this century, we might have a stable world population consistent with 2 (2.1 to be precise) surviving children for every fertile woman. In most of Europe, the figure is already lower but various parts of the world – developing countries in particular – have a long way to go. Globally speaking, population growth rates remain high. Furthermore, a rising standard of living implies an even stronger growth in the consumption of energy, water, other natural resources and food. The key question is: How will this continue and what, if anything, are we doing about it?

These observations are not new; we have known them for many years. The two most important publications on the subject are *The Limits to Growth*, a report commissioned by the Club of Rome and published in 1972, and *Our Common Future*, a 1987 report also known as the Brundtland report and issued by the United Nations. I think these are two of the most widely circulated yet worst read reports about the next phase in the evolution of our planet.

Both reports – the first from a primarily scientific and the second from a primarily political angle – set out very clearly in facts and figures the scenarios believed to be likely for the fifty years beyond 1972. Looking ahead half a century is very unusual for those in politics and business and certainly for the average citizen. As a result, relatively little was done with the reports in spite of many appeals, conferences and declarations. Many people failed to appreciate that the reports presented not predictions but scenarios – ranging from the most optimistic to the most pessimistic. Today it is all much closer.

In the meantime, 1992 saw the publication of a report entitled *Beyond the Limits*, in which the authors indicated that we were behind with measures preventing a collapse. During a conference I attended in the Netherlands in 2004, organised by the *Rijksinstituut voor Volksgezondheid en Milieuhygiëne* (Dutch Institute for Public Health and the Environment), the principal author of the Club of Rome report, Dennis Meadows, was on the programme to introduce a new publication *Limits to Growth: The 30-Year Update*. He explained that we were 'right on target' with what at the time of the first report was considered the worst conceivable scenario.

In 1984, I paid a personal visit to Meadows at Dartmouth College in the United States when I was writing my first book about evolution and our future. The message was then very clearly and convincingly explained to me by the then very young scientist and Professor of System Dynamics. The system dynamics approach addresses the inextricable interdependence of five factors in the interaction between human society and the earth's ecosystem: population size, industrial output, food production, pollution and natural resources.

Meadows's update in 2004 was 32 years after the Club of Rome report. The various scenarios he had given in 1972 indicated that, by the middle of the 21st century, there might be a major discontinuity, a collapse. We would notice relatively little in the 20th century and the first ten years of the 21st century. This explains why the original report was not only poorly read but for most people was simply too far removed from their daily lives. Now that we have already entered the second decade of the 21st century, things are different. It is not about our own future – the future of retired baby-boomers – but the future of our children and grandchildren, who had not yet been born in 1972 but who are alive now.

A new report to the Club of Rome, launched in May 2012, forecasts that by the middle of the century the world population will have stabilised at 8 billion people and 3 billion people will be living below the poverty line. At the same time, global warming will have reached disastrous levels. To prevent this scenario of collapse, the report recommends a highly centralised system of governance for decision-making purposes, citing China as an example. This seems a very unlikely and undesirable outcome to me but it is clear that our current systems need to change.

A lack of global support

The United Nations report *Our Common Future* was also distributed widely during and after 1987 and a subject of discussion everywhere. Yet at that time and for many years to come, there was not much success in producing a concrete translation to a sustainable future society, where our children's children and their children would have the same opportunity as we do today to live a quality life. The now widely known concept of 'sustainable development' was born in this report.

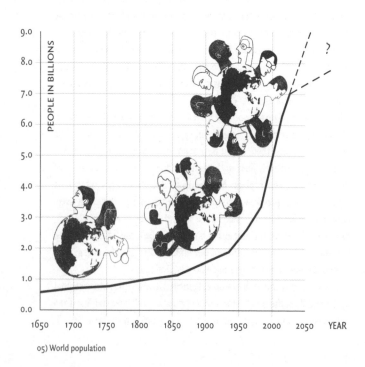

05) World population

There was again a lack of visible progress in getting structural and sustainable development off the ground notwithstanding big conferences, programmes of action, general declarations and global objectives, such as the UN Millennium Development Goals and other excellent new initiatives in the area of sustainability. The main reasons include a lack of political support, a lack of funds, indecision within the machinery of government, and a short-term corporate and political horizon in a world divided between poor developing countries, newly industrialised countries and rich countries. And then we have of course the biggest dilemma of all: a resident of Beijing aspires to the standard of living of a Londoner but the Londoner will not give it up.

We are making progress but we are very late and very slow.

The last few decades have seen real progress compared to previous decades in terms of a decrease in the use of scarce raw materials and pollution of the environment, but there are still numerous areas where substantial improvements are required to prevent – or at least alleviate – a scenario of overshoot and collapse, to use the terminology of the 1972 report. We are making progress but we are very late and very slow, perhaps not too late to limit its scale but too late to prevent it completely. The lead times are simply too long.

Despite the extensive efforts put into sustainability by governments, experts, volunteers, entrepreneurs and organisations throughout the world – and I have been right in the middle of it in the past twenty years – these efforts have not yet lived up to the promise of an effective coordinated global approach towards an imminent major discontinuity. Every region in the world has its own issues and is going through its own stage of development, determined by its own history, politics, geography, demography, economy and ecology. The failure to achieve the goals of the climate conferences in Copenhagen in 2010 and Durban in 2011 is a clear illustration of the fact that in this differentiated world order we are not yet able to create a new gobal model of decision-making.

The same can be said for the Rio+20 Earth Summit, which took place in June 2012 and was attended by 50,000 participants from 193 countries. This summit managed to set up two working groups – one on the definition of sustainable development goals and one on the costs of reaching such goals – which will report to the UN General Assembly meeting in the

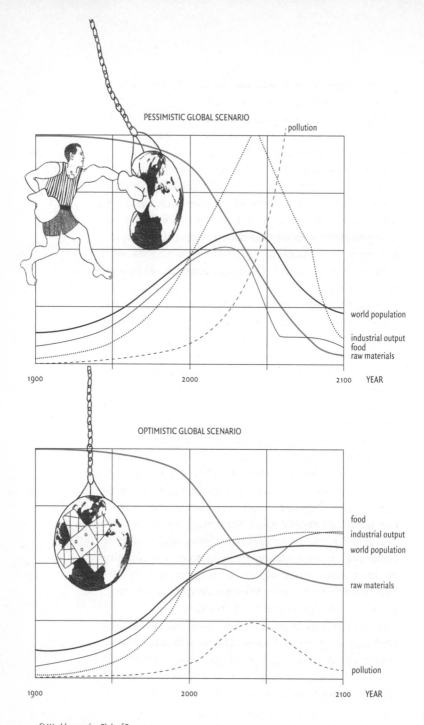

PESSIMISTIC GLOBAL SCENARIO

pollution

world population

industrial output
food
raw materials

1900   2000   2100   YEAR

OPTIMISTIC GLOBAL SCENARIO

food
industrial output
world population

raw materials

pollution

1900   2000   2100   YEAR

06) World scenarios Club of Rome 1972

autumn of 2013. But apart from this, the summit did not hammer out any sustainable development goals or agreements. Nor have we reached the end of the crises and collapses we have experienced in the last few decades. The recent global financial crisis is yet another example.

We no longer need to convince ourselves that structurally we are in trouble.

It seems an illusion to believe that we will find solutions to these issues with our conventional models. Einstein once said that you cannot solve problems with the same methodology which created them. There is no political coherence in the solutions offered to remedy the global problems we are facing. Nor is there any interconnection across professional disciplines working on such problems. The documentary evidence available has shown this over and over again. We no longer need to convince ourselves that structurally we are in trouble. We do not need to hold further conferences.

We need to convince ourselves that there are solutions. And in the past fifteen years, through my own modest programmes of action in the area of global water issues, I have discovered that a solution-oriented mentality is much more inspiring and effective than a problem-oriented mentality. Showing people images of catastrophe and misery and arousing feelings of guilt does not stimulate them. Showing them solutions, improvements and personal effort does.

The evolutionary clock keeps ticking

The problems afflicting the evolutionary phase where we find ourselves today are very much underrated. The same is true of the notion that we now play a decisive role in the process: we no longer follow a specific pattern passively but can create a pattern actively. Throughout society, there is denial. There are protests against doomsday thinking, while hopes are expressed and claims made that things are not all that bad. We human beings do not realise that it is now up to us. We live primarily in the meso world of family life, friends, work, politics, retirement – the cares and joys of today and tomorrow. Evolution is not an issue. But that is what it is ultimately all about.

Evolution is the very reason for our existence. Evolution not only has a long-term past – an interesting subject of dinner-time conversation – but there is evolution now and there will be evolution in the future. Together,

We play a decisive role in evolution; we can actively create a new pattern.

we are going through a spectacularly exciting phase after approximately 13.5 billion years of evolution and we constitute a living and decisive part of that process. How much time do we have to play our part? If I look at the scenarios for the next 25 years, then I see an evolutionary process in creation progressing towards a discontinuity which our traditional socio-economic models do not prepare us for. I am not talking about conventional problems with growth, employment, budget deficits, an ageing population, immigration or US dollar exchange rates but a radical discontinuity in the conventional growth model. This discontinuity will arise either through a fundamental change towards a sustainable model or through a collapse if the situation gets out of control. In the latter case, a sustainable model is still likely to emerge in the end but not before a great deal of misery has been incurred. My guess is that given current trends we will end up somewhere between these two scenarios.

What wisdom can the evolutionary history of our cosmos offer apart from the likelihood of another major discontinuity on the way to a new model? How will our self-reflective consciousness and solution-oriented mentality help us cope? I do not have the ultimate answer but, with some personal observations, I can give a general idea of the lessons we can learn from our evolutionary history.

A coherent pattern
The first lesson we can learn is that, based on a coherent pattern in evolution as outlined earlier, the process is not fed from without but from within by a given condition. I call this condition creation. The process is fed with information in the form of natural constants from which new choices have arisen and new forms have evolved continually over time. In the first 10 billion years, the process followed a pattern which was tight and logical, mathematical, physical and chemical, without mutation, without selection, random chance or complexity. That same condition gave rise to biological evolution in the next 3.5 billion years. This phase also followed a pattern but with many more variants. The growing complexity of phenomena was accompanied by a growing vulnerability as well as a growing level of consciousness. In this process, the elements turned more and more into participants co-steering and influencing the

process, using the same basic building blocks but with many more opportunities and choices.

Today, the human race is endowed with self-reflective consciousness, its own creativity and a co-creative role in the evolutionary process. The current, superfast phase which we are intensively nurturing ourselves from the noosphere indicates that we are good at it – we are super-creative. This is the good news. The bad news is that our self-reflective consciousness has not yet led us to design a coherent new model for the future. In our rush, the coherence that is integral to the evolutionary process has come unstuck. This is something we need to restore.

Coherence is essential in the entire process of evolution and hence in the phase where we are today. It implies that every step in the process – past and future – interacts with every internal and external factor relevant to the process. There are no isolated steps; they are all part of an integrated whole. This was also the basic principle of the system dynamics approach put forward in the Club of Rome report. From the internal organisation and efficiency of quantum particles to the functioning of organs and organisms, everything in evolution is carefully arranged according to a coherent pattern. Our heart can pump around 5 litres of blood in a complex multi-functional organism for 24 hours a day and, if we are lucky, 80 years non-stop. Our body is a striking example of built-in coherence, maintained with iron discipline and far-reaching delegation throughout the whole organism. If there is a serious malfunction somewhere, we fall sick and might even die.

If a system or model reaches its maximum level of manageability, then that system or model will fall apart. The evolutionary process will require a new model, made up of the building blocks from previous phases. If the current model of human society becomes too difficult to manage and loses its coherence, then the pattern followed by evolution suggests that the existing model will not be able to grow any further and will give way to a fundamentally new model. In the 21st century, we ourselves could design such a model from within. It would probably show completely different consumption behaviour, more conscious and sustainable use of energy, water and other natural resources by every individual, and a responsible attitude to food intake. It would also pay more attention to culture and spirituality and less to the numerous consumer goods and programmes on TV which add no value other than to satisfy a desire for

> *In the 21st century, we ourselves could design such a model from within.*

sensation and coarseness, keep up external appearances, and fill the emptiness of life.

New models, innovative outcomes

A second lesson from the history of evolution is that the given initial condition harbours the potential to generate surprising, unpredictable, sudden innovations whenever a discontinuity presents itself. In the past, this innovation 'emerged' without any build-up or prelude. Now, the situation has changed because we are conscious participants in the process, look back and ahead, observe the process and can see signs of things to come.

The explosive growth in world population and even faster growing consumption in the last one hundred years, together with the limited resources of our planet to meet such growth, the mutual disagreements within supranational organisations about alternative solutions, and the exponential development of other processes around us could all be signs of an imminent groundbreaking innovation. But are we in a position to implement and shape that innovation? Will society in the 21st century suddenly give rise to a global genius, a collective eureka? I cannot imagine this happening because mankind is still very fragmented and far from a collective organism.

Nonetheless, in the billions of years of our evolutionary past, there have been unexpected turning points on a number of occasions. The difference with today is of course that past turning points arose from an inorganic and then organic evolutionary model, while mankind has now essentially acquired the ability to create its own model and steer the outcome within the context of the spiritual phase of evolution. The computer, whose processing capacity might well exceed that of the human brain around 2035, could facilitate such a turning point.

What we can learn from the process of evolution is that any break-through will be unpredictable, surprising, and inevitable, like all other discontinuities in that process. But we would be able to steer the outcome, not – or at least, not yet – as a collective organism but as an individual organism within a larger collection.

Diversity

A third lesson from our evolutionary past is that every discontinuity and the subsequent phase usually led to the emergence of considerable diversification. We have also witnessed this after mass extinctions arising from catastrophes such as meteor strike and climate change. When existing and established ecosystems are completely overturned, niches of ecological innovation open up. It is cold comfort for those generations who will not be able to reap the benefits of these innovations. But it is a marvellous prospect for those who are still to come. And this is what the sustainable development goals are all about: the generations who will succeed us.

Individual contribution

I leave it to the reader to decide what can be done with the lessons learnt from evolution. The only advice I can give is my personal view, namely

QUANTUM COMPUTER

Brain of mankind

Brain of human individual

Brain of mouse

Brain of insect

Brain of worm

INDEX OF PROCESSING CAPACITY

1900   1920   1940   1960   1980   2000   ->   SUCCESSIVE COMPUTER GENERATIONS

07) Processing capacity of computers compared with brain of organisms

You are a subject in creation rather than an object in evolution.

that, no matter what model emerges and no matter how it emerges, everything begins with a thorough examination of our individual self: How do we see our position in the world and what role do we play from that position in the evolutionary process? It should be an examination – conducted by ourselves and not by others – of our individual role in the social order and of the contribution of that role to the coherent and disciplined functioning of a future model, from within and not from without. This is also a lesson from the evolutionary selection mechanism in developmental biology.

What I have learnt on my journey of discovery is that we should restore the coherence we have lost as individuals first, starting with ourselves in our own meso world. No government, no United Nations, no conferences and no declarations can do it for us. My strong belief in a given condition at the basis of evolution in creation means that I should be able to recover the connection with that condition through myself and not through a Creator, a government, a psychotherapist or a fortune-teller. They might be able to help us, but creation is what you are yourself. You are a subject in creation rather than an object in evolution.

This also means that solutions to the problems which we as humans are confronted with should not only be implemented from above but also from below, i.e. 'bottom up' as well as 'top down'. There is a good reason for the adage: 'If you want to change the world, you must first change yourself.' Without a convincing commitment at the bottom, an initiative imposed from above will not be feasible. For pragmatic reasons, human society will always require and display a combination of top-down and bottom-up decision-making, but if the individual is not interested in the process of decision-making then there is no hope for the process of long-term change.

In the last few decades, the projections in the reports *The Limits to Growth* and *Our Common Future* have remained relatively abstract reading and have been addressed primarily in top-down programmes, facts and figures, counter-productive bureaucracy, huge conferences and turf wars between stakeholders. Individuals have got lost and many have been withdrawing into their own meso world. All in all, the past forty years of struggling to find an effective model for sustainable development in the world have not delivered enough, while the evolutionary clock keeps ticking away.

Education and religion: under the radar

How can we give the bottom-up approach an extra boost in 21st-century society so as to generate an impulse that will lead to evolutionary innovation?

If the individual is not interested in the decision-making process then there is no hope for long-term change.

The elements in human society that could play a significant role here are groups of people who are perhaps the least obvious candidates in public opinion. Newspaper readers and television viewers mostly get images of the outside of society via the faces and statements of politicians, top civil servants, executive directors of listed companies, trade union leaders, football players and celebrities. Yet there is a whole body of generally obscure individuals who do equally important work but do not step out into the spotlight as often. They are the inside, the backbone of society.

I am referring to two important institutions, namely education and religion. Both are in direct contact with large parts of the population all over the world, and in developing countries they often go hand in hand. They differentiate themselves from two other major institutions, namely the business community and the political system, in their long-term continuity and the lack of any need to make profit or win over voters.

Educational institutions are concerned with moulding the younger generation, the generation who will populate, structure and experience the middle of the current century. Religious institutions are concerned with the connection between the meta world and the meso world of individuals, whatever their occupation or orientation. Policy makers on the world stage of politics have as yet paid little attention to these two types of institution and their role in the upheaval which can be expected in the structures of 21st-century society.

Educational institutions can play a key role by informing young people about the challenges which we will be facing in the next 25 years. If teachers can keep away from the supposed conflict between science and religion and make information easily accessible through text and illustration, then they will offer a major source of inspiration for young people to become involved and dedicate themselves to a clear and important joint cause.

This will require a globally coordinated approach to communicating a detailed and accurate picture of the current evolutionary phase and our role as human beings, a picture that could well fit in with different philosophies and religions and thus would actually reinforce their mission. Any such project will be very costly, a candidate perhaps for a large private endowment. An excellent example is the Big History project of the Melinda and Bill Gates Foundation (www.bighistoryproject.com), which is developing a history of evolution curriculum for 9th grade students throughout the world.

Then there are the various religions, or faith institutions. The eleven most important in the world are large enough to put them on a par with the world's oldest and biggest multinational corporations. Unlike commercial multinationals, most of these religious institutions have existed for more than 2000 years, do not have short-term agendas and do not operate under a profit motive. Together they own and manage more than six per cent of all the world's usable land (including agriculture and forestry) and institutional investments.

In the past the Roman Catholic Church, in particular, contributed to the dichotomy between thinking styles in the arts and sciences. The Jesuit Teilhard de Chardin broke through that dichotomy in the last century and recent statements by the pope suggest that today his vision is increasingly being adopted by the Vatican. The separation between religion and science as well as between religion and nature is growing less pronounced. In the last decade, virtually all religions have started to realise that preserving the integrity of creation, including nature, should get far more attention in religious practice. The soul of the earth should get as much attention as the human soul.

Although in the course of history many wars and wrongs have arisen from the social involvement and ideological position of religious institutions, they have over the centuries nonetheless remained strong bastions in human society all over the world.

At an international gathering in November 2009, representatives of eleven of the main religions each presented their formal seven-year plan for the conservation of nature with programmes of action from their members. The conference theme was 'Many Heavens, One Earth'. The project was coordinated by the Alliance of Religions and Conservation in the United Kingdom, a secular organisation uniting eleven religions (ARC and www.arcworld.org). The presentation took place at Windsor

Castle in the presence of Prince Philip, founder of ARC in 1995, and UN Secretary General Ban Ki-Moon. A colourful contingent of high-ranking delegates together represented all the religions.

> *The soul of the earth should get as much attention as the human soul.*

Above the radar

Education and religion have generally stayed under the radar in terms of their potential to put into practice the bottom-up approach to a societal turnaround. But their potential is enormous.

This potential does not alter the fact that those individuals around the world who are not affiliated with a religion and are no longer being educated will be able to play an important role. They are however a diffuse and elusive group, in fact a group I belong to myself. This is also true for the environmental conservation organisations, which despite being relatively small are very effective.

Nor does it alter the fact that the business and political communities will continue to put considerable effort into developing the technological and social innovations needed to foster a sustainable society. But we can hardly expect from these organisations that they will make sweeping changes in the short run to address the discontinuity expected in 25 years' time. To survive, they need paying customers and voting constituents in the short term.

If educational and religious institutions can effect a reversal in thinking and acting from within, bottom-up and on a micro scale by stimulating individual responsibility, then we might be able to engineer a favourable discontinuity on a macro scale in the current century. It will mean a fundamental change in our current socio-economic system, which is based on quantitative growth whereas the new model will be based on qualitative growth. This is indeed a major discontinuity.

The new story

My personal opinion is that this reversal from quantity to quality cannot be realised unless we first – on an individual basis – rediscover the link between our personal meso world, the macro world, the micro world and especially the meta world. After all, these four worlds are inextricably connected. An awareness and experience of that connectedness can greatly help an individual recognise opportunities to play a part in restoring the coherence we have lost ecologically, socially and spiritually.

The spiritual angle – that of the meta world – individuals can interpret in their own way, based on their own feeling or experience, be it religious or non-religious, with or without a name. When people free up time for such matters, they might consciously be motivated to keep the planet liveable in our century. The space and time made available by being less obsessed with the material meso world can be applied to the meta world. And this will be essential to make people aware that we must change our behaviour in the next 25 years if we are to give effect to the notion of sustainability.

It simply means a halt to population growth, sustainable consumption of water, energy and food, and the integration of production and waste through full-scale recycling. None of this is new and there are hundreds of websites with information on how individuals can contribute. But not enough is being done at present because there is no good example of a process which creates awareness and convinces and inspires people to change their behaviour. This will only happen when there is proper communication of the new story on where we now stand in the superfast process of evolution, a process which – if we are not careful – could surprise us with a new discontinuity.

I have tried to convince the reader that we can make a constructive effort and prepare ourselves for that story by consciously and convincingly reconnecting the four worlds in and through which we live, by querying the major mysteries in creation, and by allowing ourselves to be inspired by the dynamics of evolution – in eternity and time.

Today's and tomorrow's younger generations are ready to acquire such a state of mind and many young people are looking for a new story, a story which they will realise themselves in their own way. They now have ample concrete reason for taking individual action. Whether this will happen and how will be a key determinant in the next 25 years.

Who was Teilhard?

Pierre Teilhard de Chardin was born in France on 1 May 1881. He joined the Jesuit Order in 1899, studied geology and palaeontology, and became a world-renowned authority in his field of expertise. He was not an armchair scholar but a practical man. He was a stretcher bearer at the front lines during Word War I, carried out archaeological research in China for 25 years (his name is linked to the discovery of *Homo erectus pekinensis*, among other things) and produced a vast body of scientific work.

His merit as a philosopher lies in the fact that he brought together scientific, religious, social and mystical thinking under a single banner in his magnum opus in the field of evolutionary theory. He was confronted with fundamental opposition from the Roman Catholic Church, culminating in the encyclical *Humani Generis* of Pope Pius XII (1950), a publication which was undeniably directed at Teilhard's theories of evolution and which more or less stated that any thought not in line with the views of Thomas Aquinas (13th century) was prohibited. It was Teilhard's timely decision to leave his works to his secretary Jeanne Mortier which made publication possible after his death in 1955.

The scientific community too levied a barrage of criticism against his views and writings. He advanced hypotheses about the past and future of life and mankind which did not stand up to critical scientific scrutiny: they could not be demonstrated and were rooted in mysticism.

In the 1960s, however, both science and the Church grew closer to his vision. Specifically, during the Second Ecumenical Council of the Vatican, a new attitude can be discerned in the *Gaudium et Spes: Pastoral Constitution on the Church in the Modern World* (1965). The introductory statement includes the following observation: 'History itself speeds along on so rapid a course that an individual person can scarcely keep abreast of it. The destiny of the human community has become all of a piece, where once the various groups of men had a kind of private history of their own. Thus, the human race has passed from a rather static concept of reality to a more dynamic, evolutionary one. In consequence there has arisen a new series of problems, a series as numerous as can be, calling for efforts of analysis and synthesis.'

That a new attitude has continued to exert an effect is clear from two recent conferences. One was organised by the Vatican in November 2008 at the Pontifical Academy of Sciences, where an international group of scientists and theologians gathered together. The conference topic was 'Scientific Insights into the Evolution of the Universe and of Life'. The second took place in March 2009 at the Pontifical Gregorian University, where the main theme was 'Biological Evolution: Facts and Theories'. Both conferences examined many of the subjects treated in the present book. A reading of the presentations makes clear that, in this scholarly environment, learning brings with it more questions than answers. It is worth noting that the conference papers no longer look for extreme confrontation – as was the case with Galilei and subsequently Teilhard – but explore the interface between science and religion.

This turnaround began with Pope Paul VI's 1965 encyclical letter *Gaudium et Spes* and was followed much later – in Aosta in October 1996 – by a statement from John Paul II that science had shown evolution to be more than a hypothesis. Pope Benedict XVI too has issued statements along these lines. During the celebration of Vespers in Aosta on 24 July 2009, he praised Teilhard de Chardin's views on cosmogenesis.

The achievement of a synthesis between elements inherent in the arts and the sciences should be seen in the broader context of the evolution of a living cosmos. In his principal work on evolution, Teilhard gives a comprehensive description of the evolutionary process, very likely – and increasingly likely – capturing the process as it actually unfolded. Since the time when he put together his account, between 1938 and 1940, much more new scientific material has become available. The descriptive aspect of his work therefore requires some major updating. Even so, recent insights generated by astrophysics reinforce his ideas on the evolution of the universe.

An essential aspect of Teilhard's thinking finds expression in his interpretation of the story of Genesis. Here he saw the idea of an evolving dynamic universe: *cosmogenesis*, or the notion that the entire universe is in a dynamic state of creative flux with all components interacting and interconnected. This contrasts with the traditional interpretation of Genesis, which assumes an unchanging universe. It should be clear that Teilhard's world view does not admit any radical dualism.

Other important elements in his work are as follows. First, it demonstrates the existence of a cosmic evolutionary process since the Big Bang and before the emergence of life. Second, he had the courage and vision needed to posit and substantiate the hypothesis that the process is moving in an irreversible direction, ever forward towards a specific goal. The dynamic link between earth, mankind and universe is described most clearly in *Le Milieu Divin* (1957) (*The Divine Milieu*). In this work, Teilhard emphasises the notion that humans cannot be seen separately from earth. They are part of the earth rather than on earth. And because the earth is part of the universe, they are also part of the universe. According to the principle of cosmogenesis, the universe unfolds relentlessly and with a purpose into new and creative forms. This model is very important because human existence acquires significance in a cosmological process rather than as a life on earth on a sinful sojourn in a material world which we have to endure until we are redeemed.

In the course of a human life, Teilhard sees a shift in focus from attachment to detachment, and from the material to the non-material, in preparation of the transition from the material phase during life to the non-material phase after death.

Teilhard's realisation that there is unity and coherence in evolution and creation constitutes the link with the Taoist view of the world. Both transcend compartmental thinking. An essential aspect is that the material evolution from atom to human organism proceeded extremely slowly, taking billions of years, while the non-material evolution currently well under way – without any genetic transfer – has led to exponential change within just a few generations. The change is occurring much faster than can be handled by the traditional social, economic and political structures which govern society. This is creating major challenges.

Teilhard sees the rapidly intensifying interaction within human society as a clear, new evolutionary phase leading from individual consciousness to a higher degree of planetary consciousness. It is the result of the explosion in communication through travel, radio, and television and – unbeknownst to him at the time – of the breath-taking acceleration in transnational communication made possible by GPS and internet.

The interconnectedness between the inorganic geosphere (earth), the organic biosphere (life on earth) and the spiritual noosphere (the mental reservoir of mankind) in the evolutionary process of the earth leads Teilhard to the notion that the noosphere will continue to grow in both size and quality. The noosphere is undergoing explosive growth and will result in a new dimension in the evolution of mankind, with completely new relationships and characteristics. The outcome will be unpredictable, very much like earlier periods when nobody could have predicted the emergence of life, consciousness and self-reflective consciousness.

Whether this dimension will be attained now depends on mankind itself, in other words the individual and society. In this respect, Teilhard strongly emphasises the responsibility and freedom of the individual to steer the process and give it substance. He assumes that the new 'collective mind' will strengthen the character of the individual without 'submerging' him.

What are models?

This book often refers to the concept of a 'model'. What does this term mean? A model is by definition not the same as reality. It is a simplified picture invented by the human mind, a schematic representation of a natural phenomenon, of a scientific observation or of just an impression. A model is never complete and therefore never fully coherent. But it satisfies the human desire to discover order and regularity in the structure and dynamics of nature, which then does seem complete and coherent.

A model is usually applicable to a piece of reality. So a model represents our perception of a part of reality but is not reality itself. We do not know what reality is. We do know, for instance, what a chair is but not how the image of a chair reaches us from atoms and molecules – models as well! – and emerges in our consciousness via the neural circuits in the brain and the filtering carried out through the senses.

A perfect example of how we literally 'imagine' reality is when we think something has a colour even though, upon further consideration, that something does not *have* a colour but *gives rise* to a colour under certain conditions. That something does not show any colour at all when it is dark. Colour emerges from white light shining onto that something, for example a flower. The flower absorbs specific wavelengths from the white light and reflects certain wavelengths. So a dye is not a substance with colour but a composition which absorbs some and reflects other wavelengths. Through reflection that something returns a colour which corresponds with the reflected wavelengths. No object shows a colour if there is no light shining on it. Wavelengths which can 'escape' from white light are as old as the emergence of the universe. So colour was not a new phenomenon when coloured things emerged during evolution. The concept of colour emerged from the Big Bang.

This analysis is full of 'models' invented by humans, such as the concepts of 'wavelength', 'white light' and 'dye'. Then there is also the question of whether we all see the same colour or whether this depends on the individual. We may be talking about the same colour, but perhaps we do not see the same colour.

It is clear that the application of models has given us much knowledge which we have been able to use to study creation, discover evolution, develop technologies, increase our standard of living as well as look after and restore our health. But they remain no more than models. The only reality is creation and that is something we are ourselves.

Sources of inspiration

I am grateful to Johann Sebastian Bach, Pierre Lecomte du Noüy, Pierre Teilhard de Chardin, Loren Eiseley and Thomas Berry for their posthumous legacy of ideas, which first triggered my interest in the evolution of the cosmos and the role of mankind. Bach I got to know through his wonderful music, which carries me off to the meta world.

Tom Berry is the only source I knew in person as a friend and counsellor. We had many discussions at his home in Riverdale, NY, overlooking the Hudson River.

In Bonaire, where I wrote most of this book, I benefited greatly from conversations with Esther Wolfs and Marlene Robinson. In 2010, I met Maja Nijessen there, who as a fully qualified journalist gave me invaluable advice on how to make the manuscript more readable. She put me on to Rosa Vitalie, who was captivated by the subject and made beautiful illustrations to accompany the text exactly as I had always hoped for.

Loli Lindner closely observed the emergence of this book for more than 25 years and gave me tremendous support on my journey of discovery.

The translator responsible for the English manuscript, Ivette Jans, turned out to be more than a translator. Her critical questions about substance have enhanced the quality of the manuscript, including the Dutch original, considerably. Many improvements are due to Mark Muth in London, who betrayed his Oxford background with comments on language as well as substance.

Lia Otterspeer, who has worked for me and my foundations for twenty years, kept track of the continually changing text and lay-out with incredible dedication. I am very grateful to her.

I am also grateful to Martin Palmer for introducing me to my agent Susan Mears. She saw that Michael Mann was interested in the manuscript, which led to its publication by Watkins Publishing House, part of Duncan Baird. It was a surprising coincidence that my first book *The Transformation Factor: Towards Ecological Consciousness* was published by Element Books, a company founded by Michael.

Many thanks go to all of these individuals for helping me with their heads as well as their hearts.

Bonaire, 2013

Bibliography

Aquinas, Thomas, *Summa Contra Gentiles*. Trans. A. Pegis, J. Anderson, V. Bourke and C. O'Neill, 1955. Rpt. Notre Dame: University of Notre Dame Press, 1975

Aquinas, Thomas, *Summa Theologiae*. Cambridge: Blackfriars, New York: McGraw-Hill, 1964-1973

Beenakker, Carlo W.J., *Magische Technologie (Magic Technology)*. Haarlem: Koninklijke Hollandsche Maatschappij der Wetenschappen, 2008

Behe, Michael J., *The Edge of Evolution: The Search for the Limits of Darwinism*. New York: Simon & Schuster, Inc., 2007

Blackmore, Susan, *Consciousness: A Very Short Introduction*. Oxford, New York: Oxford University Press, 2005

Chaisson, Eric, *Epic of Evolution: Seven Ages of the Cosmos*. New York: Columbia University Press, 2005

Chang, Chung-Yuan, *Tao: A New Way of Thinking*. New York: Harper & Row, 1975

Collins, Francis S., *The Language of God: A Scientist Presents Evidence for Belief*. London, New York: Free Press, 2006

Daleux, André, *Teilhard de Chardin: Science et Foi Réconciliées? (Teilhard de Chardin: Science and Religion Reconciled?)* Saint Jean de Valériscle: Editions GabriAndre, 2001

Damasio, Antonio, *Het Zelf Wordt Zich Bewust: Hersenen, Bewustzijn, Ik.* Amsterdam: Wereldbibliotheek, 2010 (*Self Comes to Mind: Constructing the Conscious Brain.* New York: Pantheon Books, 2010)

Darwin, Charles, *On the Origin of Species.* London: Allen Lane Penguin Books, 2010

Davies, Paul, *The Eerie Silence: Are We Alone in the Universe?* London: Allen Lane, 2010

Dawkins, Richard, *The Greatest Show on Earth.* New York: Free Press, 2009

Fodor, Jerry and Massimo Piattelli-Palmarini, *What Darwin Got Wrong.* London: Profile Books Ltd, 2010

Gaudium et Spes, Second Vatican Ecumenical Council, Session IX, 1965

Gazziniga, Michael S., *Human: The Science Behind What Makes Us Unique.* New York: Harper Collins Publishers, 2008

Gilding, Paul, *The Great Disruption: How the Climate Crisis Will Transform the Global Economy.* London, Berlin, New York, Sydney: Bloomsbury, 2011

Graham. A.C., *Chuang Tzu: The Inner Chapters.* London: George Allen & Unwin, 1981

Hawking, Stephen and Leonard Mlodinow, *The Grand Design.* London: Bantam Press, 2010

Ho, Mae-Wan, *The Rainbow and the Worm: The Physics of Organism.* London: World Scientific Publishing Co., 2008

Jaspers, Karl, *Vom Ursprung und Ziel der Geschichte.* Munich: Piper und Co., 1949 (*The Origin and Goal of History.* Trans. Michael Bullock. New Haven: Yale University Presss, 1953)

Kurzweil, Ray, *The Singularity is Near: When Humans Transcend Biology.* New York: Penguin Group USA, 2005

Lecomte du Noüy, Pierre, *Human Destiny.* New York: Signet Books by The New American Library of World Literature, Inc., 1947

Le Fanu, James, *Why Us? How Science Rediscovered the Mystery of Ourselves.* New York: Pantheon Books, 2009

Meadows, Donella H., Dennis L. Meadows, Jørgen Randers and William W. Behrens III, *The Limits to Growth*. New York: New American Library, 1972

Meadows, Donella H., Dennis L. Meadows and Jørgen Randers, *Beyond the Limits: Confronting Global Collapse, Envisioning a Sustainable Future*. White River Junction: Chelsea Green Publishing Co., 1992

Meadows, Donella H., Dennis L. Meadows and Jørgen Randers, *Limits to Growth: The 30-Year Update*. London: Earthscan, 2005

Melsen, A.G.M. van, *Geloof, Wetenschap en Maatschappelijke Omwentelingen*. (*Religion, Science and Social Upheaval*.) In: Katholiek Studiecentrum, 1977

Monod, J., *Le Hasard et la Nécessité*. Paris: Editions du Seuil, 1964 (*Chance and Necessity*. Trans. A. Wainhouse. New York: Vintage Books, 1972)

Nadeau, Robert and Menas Kafatos, *The Non-Local Universe: The New Physics and Matters of the Mind*. New York: Oxford University Press, 1999

Pope Pius XII, *Humani Generis: Encyclical Letter of Pope Pius XII*. New York: Paulist Press, 1950

Potter, Christopher, *You are Here: A Portable History of the Universe*. New York: HarperCollins Publishers, 2009

Randers, Jørgen, *2052: A Global Forecast for the Next Forty Years*. White River Junction: Chelsea Green Publishing Co., 2012

Ricard, Matthieu and Trinh Xuan Thuan, *The Quantum and the Lotus*. New York: Three Rivers Press, 2001

Rousseau, J.J., *Discours sur l'Origine et les Fondements de l'Inégalité Parmi les Hommes*. 1755 (*Discourse on the Origin and Foundation of Inequality Among Men*. Trans. H. Rosenblatt. New York: Bedford/St. Martins, 2011)

Rousseau, J.J., *Du Contrat Social ou Principe du Droit Politique*. 1762 (*The Social Contract*. Trans. G.D.H. Cole. Stilwel: Digireads.com Publishing, 2005)

Schrödinger, Erwin, *What is Life? The Physical Aspect of the Living Cell*. London: Cambridge University Press, 1962

Sheldrake, Rupert, *A New Science of Life: The Hypothesis of Formative Causation*. Los Angeles: J.P Tarcher, Inc., 1981

Stikker, Allerd, *Over Vrouw en Man: De Onverbrekelijke Samenhang.* Amsterdam, Antwerp: Kopperlith & Co, 2000 (*Closing the Gap: Exploring the History of Gender Relations.* Amsterdam: Amsterdam University Press, 2002)

Stikker, Allerd, *Sustainability and Business Management.* In: Business Strategy and the Environment, I(3), 1992, pp. 1-8

Stikker, Allerd, *Tao, Teilhard en Westers Denken.* Amsterdam: Bres, 1986 (*The Transformation Factor: Towards Ecological Consciousness.* Rockport MA, London, Brisbane: Element Books, 1992)

Stikker, Allerd, *Water: The Blood of the Earth.* New York: Cosimo Books, 2007

Strawson, Galen et al., *Consciousness and its Place in Nature: Does Physicalism Entail Panpsychism?* Ed. Anthony Freeman. Exeter: Imprint Academic, 2006

Teilhard de Chardin, Pierre, *Le Phénomène Humain.* Paris: Editions du Seuil, 1955 (*The Phenomenon of Man.* London: William Collins Sons & Co., Ltd.; New York: Harper & Brothers, 1959)

Teilhard de Chardin, Pierre, *Le Milieu Divin.* Paris: Editions du Seuil, 1957 (*The Divine Milieu.* London: William Collins Sons & Co., Ltd.; New York: Harper & Brothers, 1960)

The World Commission on Environment and Development, *Our Common Future.* Oxford, New York: Oxford University Press, 1987

Thompson, D'Arcy Wentworth, *On Growth and Form.* Ed. John Tyler Bonner. Cambridge: Cambridge University Press, 1961

Universe or Multiverse? Ed. Bernard Carr. London: Cambridge University Press, 2007